ACCELERATE
YOUR
REAL ESTATE

ACCELERATE YOUR REAL ESTATE

Build a Hands-Off BRRRR Rental Portfolio with the SCALE Strategy

Palak Shah and Niti Jamdar

This publication is protected under the U.S. Copyright Act of 1976 and all other applicable international, federal, state, and local laws, and all rights are reserved, including resale rights: You are not allowed to reproduce, transmit, or sell this book in part or in full without the written permission of the publisher.

Limit of Liability: Although the author and publisher have made reasonable efforts to ensure that the contents of this book were correct at press time, the author and publisher do not make, and hereby disclaim, any representations and warranties regarding the content of the book, whether express or implied, including implied warranties of merchantability or fitness for a particular purpose. You use the contents in this book at your own risk. Author and publisher hereby disclaim any liability to any other party for any loss, damage, or cost arising from or related to the accuracy or completeness of the contents of the book, including any errors or omissions in this book, regardless of the cause. Neither the author nor the publisher shall be held liable or responsible to any person or entity with respect to any loss or incidental, indirect, or consequential damages caused, or alleged to have been caused, directly or indirectly, by the contents contained herein. The contents of this book are informational in nature and are not legal or tax advice, and the authors and publishers are not engaged in the provision of legal, tax or any other advice. You should seek your own advice from professional advisors, including lawyers and accountants, regarding the legal, tax, and financial implications of any real estate transaction you contemplate.

Accelerate Your Real Estate: Build a Hands-Off Rental Portfolio with the SCALE Strategy
Palak Shah and Niti Jamdar

Published by BiggerPockets Publishing LLC, Denver, CO
Copyright © 2023 by Palak Shah and Niti Jamdar
All rights reserved.

ISBN: 9781960178114 (ebook)
ISBN: 9781960178237 (paperback)

Published in the United States of America

DEDICATION

To our children,

You are the reason we questioned the status quo. You are the reason we chose a different path. May it inspire you to dream big, explore new worlds, and never stop learning.

Love always,
Mama and Papa

Contents

CHAPTER ONE: From the Corporate Grind to a $1 Million Portfolio in One Year ... 1

CHAPTER TWO: Why Real Estate? ... 7

CHAPTER THREE: How We Defined Our Real Estate Investing Strategy ... 11

CHAPTER FOUR: Introducing the Scale Framework for BRRRR ... 23

CHAPTER FIVE: Scalable Acquisitions and Deal Analysis (a.k.a. Buy) ... 29

CHAPTER SIX: Construction that Scales (Rehab) ... 47

CHAPTER SEVEN: Adding Cash Flow (Rent) ... 65

CHAPTER EIGHT: Leverage and Commercial Financing (Refinance) ... 81

CHAPTER NINE: Exponential Growth (Repeat) ... 101

CHAPTER TEN: Taking Action with the Able Framework ... 117

CHAPTER ELEVEN: Balancing Social Impact and Profitability ... 135

CHAPTER TWELVE: Adopting the Mindset of a Successful Investor ... 141

CHAPTER THIRTEEN: Planning for the Future ... 151

Fast Forward ... 165

Acknowledgments ... 167

About the Authors ... 169

Thank You ... 171

CHAPTER ONE

From the Corporate Grind to a $1 Million Portfolio in One Year

It was a typical Wednesday morning. We were getting our two-year-old ready for preschool, making breakfast, packing lunches, getting dressed, and trying to be quiet so as not to wake up our three-month-old baby—you know, the usual, chaotic working day with young kids.

Niti made a two-egg omelet with cheese, "extra-golden," just as our daughter likes it. We sat down around the kitchen counter. My news interrupted our usual ten minutes of quiet before the daily chaos resumes.

"So, I talked to my new boss yesterday. I asked if there is any way I could work from home two days a week," I said.

"What did he say?" Niti asked.

"It's not going to be possible. And starting Monday, he wants me to work at a different engineering plant, which is an hour and a half drive each way," I responded wistfully.

"Well, what are you going to do?" Niti inquired.

I didn't have an answer. It wasn't supposed to be like this.

Growing up in India, I lost my dad when I was five years old. My mom ran the house on her teacher's salary, but it wasn't enough to make ends meet. So, she started a few side-businesses to supplement our income. Watching her work tirelessly to provide me with the best education and upbringing, I felt the weight of her expectations from a young age. I didn't want to let her hard work and sacrifice go in vain. So, I got focused.

I learned to follow society's prescribed "steps for success," becoming the top-ranked student for every grade in school and earning an undergraduate engineering degree. I then moved to the U.S. and obtained a master's in Mechanical Engineering from the University of Illinois at Chicago. After that, for seventeen years, I climbed the corporate ladder, became an expert in my field and traveling all over the world, presenting to C-suite executives of companies.

I waited until my mid-thirties to have a baby so I could pursue my career aspirations, thinking that by then, I would have enough financial stability to be able to spend a lot of time with my kids. I thought that my five-year, high-performer track record with the company would give me some flexibility when my kids were young.

I was wrong.

I made the best case I could, highlighting the value of my contributions and the time and dedication I had poured into my work up to that point. I even crafted a game plan on to remain as productive as before. I was hoping, at the very least, to have the option of working a few days from home. But when I needed it most, my job offered me zero flexibility, and instead, my boss asked me to spend more time away from my kids.

Later that day, I was in my office, pumping breast milk for my newborn, when it dawned on me: I'd been sold a lie. Despite being in a high position, I felt like a tiny cog in a giant machine—insignificant, small, and easily replaceable. Where was the corporate ladder really taking me? The higher I climbed, the more hours of my life would be chained to the company.

I wanted out.

"Are you okay? What are you planning to tell your boss?" Niti asked that night.

"I'm going to tell him I'm resigning," I said in a soft but firm voice. Something inside me had shifted.

Niti, who worked as a strategy and finance executive at a Fortune 100 company, had built a diverse skill set in finance, accounting, corporate strategy, and technology. Naturally, he was selected for a leadership track early on in his career. But he had made many sacrifices along the way, like so many others in corporate America. He worked more hours than required, spent a year in a different city for work, and often missed out on family time.

Like most nine-to-five employees, Niti believed that the higher he climbed the corporate ladder, the better his life would be. However, the salary increases each year failed to reflect his growing responsibilities. And with increased responsibilities came mounting stress levels, longer workdays, and an unsettling sense of uncertainty whenever the company underwent are organization.

It all came to a head when our son was born. Those of us who focus on our careers go where the opportunities are, and they are rarely in our backyard. As the adage goes, "It takes a village to raise children." A lot of us don't have that village because we moved to wherever our jobs took us. When our son was born, our daughter was twenty-two months old. Our parents lived overseas, and we didn't have reliable childcare.

To make matters worse, an important project at Niti's company coincided with our son's birth, leaving him with just one-and-a-half weeks of paternity leave despite his high performance and over a decade of service to the company. That was it!

Neither of us wanted to ever be in such a position. And that was the proverbial straw that broke the camel's back. This experience made us realize that our priorities needed to shift, and we began to consider alternative career paths that would allow us to prioritize our family while still pursuing our passions.

Niti said to me, "I want to put myself in the position where no one ever tells me how much time I can spend with my family."

So, my husband and I decided to become a single-income family. This was a difficult decision, given how much time and effort both of us put into our careers, but we agreed that it would be best if I resigned from my job so that I could spend more time with the kids and also start building our real estate portfolio. The plan was to make work optional for Niti in the future as well.

At this point, you might be wondering how I got the idea to invest in real estate. Well, it wasn't a singular eureka moment, and as you'll learn in the next chapter, we did our research and played the long game.

Even though we lived a comfortable lifestyle, I was financially prudent when it came to our monthly paychecks. I had been keeping track of all our tax returns, our budget for vacations, and our household expenditure all these years.

I put together our savings and invested it in a 25 percent down payment for a rent-ready property. My investment paid off—the rent was more than enough to pay off the monthly loan repayments. When I cleared out my office, I had two rental properties. Naturally, the idea of scaling up my real estate investments seemed like the best path forward. After all, this was a profession that offered flexibility to accommodate a working mother.

Niti and I took to real estate like it was the subject of our honors thesis. At night, we would "relax and unwind" by listening to podcasts by industry leaders, and we absorbed their insights about how we, as novices, could enter the market and become successful. We devoured several books and followed industry blogs with a kind of religious fervor.

As I mentioned, Niti was a strategy and finance executive. And his superpower is figuring out how to scale a business. The challenge with buying rental properties was the $60,000–$70,000 down payments we would need, requiring us to save up $60,000–$70,000 each time we bought a property. This would be quite difficult on a single income.

It was a slow and calculated approach. On the one hand, with two children's futures to plan for, we didn't want to rush in blindly. Our primary focus was expanding the knowledge base. On the other hand, I was also keen to leverage the technical expertise and skill set I had acquired over the years. Why not make the most of the insights I had shared with those CEOs? In the end, that was the secret weapon that allowed me to build and scale my portfolio at a much faster rate than other people who entered the scene at the same time.

I knew that there would be a certain amount of risk involved. Even with the best strategy and research, there is always the possibility of losing money on an investment. I also knew that risk-taking is an acquired skill. Our nine-to-five jobs teach us many things, but they also make us very risk-averse. The steady paycheck gives us a sense of calm, and it can be very difficult to step out of your comfort zone. It was one of the biggest mindset shifts Niti and I had to make—getting comfortable with taking risks.

Fast-forward five years, and we've built a $10 million cash-flowing real estate portfolio. Niti has quit his job and joined the business full-time, and we spend five hours a week on growing our portfolio by $3 million each year. And the best part? We have the freedom to spend as much time as we want with our kids! Not only has real estate given us the financial stability we were seeking, but it has also provided us with time and location freedom. We plan to travel three to four months every year to new countries, giving our kids the most priceless gift there is—spending time as a family. We finally have control over our own destiny, and we are not at the mercy of a corporation deciding what we are worth. To us, this is the definition of financial freedom.

What does financial freedom mean to you? We don't expect a definitive answer to this question. If we ask you this question again in five years, your answer might be slightly or even radically different.

Our ideas of what financial freedom means may differ, but we want to be clear about one thing.

Financial freedom is not just a pipe dream.

Yes, it takes time, patience, and perseverance. But it is attainable if you have the right strategy and the right execution. If this idea seems a tad scary but exciting to you, then you're in the right place. And if you think you can't do it, our goal here is to help you change that.

We are passionate about helping others obtain financial freedom through real estate and making their nine-to-five jobs optional. In the last three years, we've coached thousands of investors on how they can invest in real estate and grow a real estate portfolio.

One of the most intimidating aspects of building a real estate portfolio is finding the time to learn and implement everything, especially when juggling a busy job and young kids. And there is one thing that is even more important than money: time.

When we started investing in real estate, we were clear that we didn't want another nine-to-five job, nor did we want to spend sixty hours a week working on real estate. Instead, we leveraged the SCALE framework to build a $10 million portfolio in just four years, dedicating only about five hours of work per week. In this book, we will share how you achieve similar results.

Archimedes said, "Give me a lever long enough, and a fulcrum on which to place it, and I shall move the world."

Real estate investing isn't about simply putting in long hours on the jobsite or mastering every skill related to the trade. Isn't not even about the capital you bring. Financial freedom through real estate investing is about knowing where the fulcrum lies and which lever to use to move the world.

We developed the SCALE strategy to help guide investors on how they can grow wealth through real estate by working smarter, not harder.

This book will teach you everything you need to know to scale your portfolio to the point where you can quit your job and live on the passive income stream it generates You will learn our SCALE framework, which has allowed us to scale our assets fast while reducing our risk, all while working less than five hours a week.

To make sure you're able to execute your strategy, we will also cover essential knowledge on systems, processes, and strategic outsourcing. Our goal is to give you the tools you need to start investing and get faster results. We'll also explore how to approach retirement planning and balance social impact with profitability.

Whether you're a new real estate investor or you already have skin in the game, this book will answer two key questions:

1. *How can I transition from the corporate grind to owning a multi-million-dollar real estate portfolio within a few years, without dedicating full-time effort to the business?*
2. *What are the strategies to scale my real estate portfolio without having significant capital or relinquishing equity?*

And hopefully, you'll find the answers to some questions you haven't even consciously thought about. In short, the following chapters are a roadmap to building the life of your dreams by investing in real estate.

Are you ready to take control of your financial future?

> ### MEET ROCKSTAR INVESTOR LAURA
>
> Laura was a manager for a large corporation and a mom of two kids under five. On paper, she appeared to have it all—a well-paying job and a family she loved. However, her demanding work schedule left her with little time to spend with her kids. She was only able to see them for an hour in the morning and two hours in the evening before their bedtime.
>
> She was trying to break free from the proverbial "golden handcuffs" of corporate life. She spent her already limited free time going to walkthroughs with her real estate agent on weekends, analyzing deals without a clear direction, and jumping from one idea to the next.
>
> Laura was motivated and hardworking, and she had climbed the ladder fast that everyone around her saw her as a high achiever. The fact that she couldn't crack the code on scaling a real estate portfolio was maddening to her. As a classic Type a personality, Laura is smart as a cookie, ambitious, and focused on achieving both personal and professional success.
>
> But something Laura lacked was a methodical approach and strategy to building her portfolio as well as execution that fit her nine-to-fiver, mom lifestyle. Within a couple of months of executing the SCALE Framework, Laura closed her first deal. Within a year, she had scaled up to a $1 million portfolio. She has now invested in multiple states and enjoys spending more time with her kids than ever before. It is possible!

CHAPTER TWO
Why Real Estate?

As a new single-income family with a double-income lifestyle, we spent hours each night (after our kids were asleep) researching various business ideas. There are so many different ways to replicate a nine-to-five income. We considered selling products on Amazon or acquiring a restaurant, and we even tried to sell art online. But none of these worked, either because demanded a significant time commitment of forty to sixty hours a week, or due to the low barrier entry of an already-saturated market.

We were clear from the beginning that we didn't want to create another nine-to-five job for ourselves. Burnout among small business owners is all too common, and we didn't want to trade the frying pan of our corporate job for the fire of entrepreneurship. We understood that building a business takes work, but we were determined to create something that would allow us to stop trading hours for dollars and be able to generate passive income.

We had to find a way to make our money work for us. Investing turned out to be a clear winner because it not only provides financial freedom, but it also offers time and location freedom, which is exactly what we were after. Now, there are multiple ways to invest, but the stock market and real estate investing were our top two contenders because they have been proven over time.

LOW RETURN ON INVESTMENT WITH STOCKS

Most investment pros can't beat the stock market. In fact, according to an S&P SPIVA report, almost 90 percent of actively managed investment funds failed to beat the market over a fifteen-year period. This suggests that even seasoned investors can't get better returns than the S&P.

Therefore, a safe way to invest in stocks would be investing in an

S&P index fund. However, the average returns for S&P index fund over the last twenty years have been less than 10 percent. This means that if we invested in an S&P index fund, it would take us thirty-plus years to attain financial freedom. And we certainly did not want to wait that long!

THE EMOTIONAL STRAIN OF STOCK MARKET VOLATILITY

Some investors fail to consider the emotional roller coaster that awaits them on the stock market. Yet, when you look at charts, prices may rise and fall any second. We experienced this with our 401k, which would rise and fall periodically due to the volatility in the stock market, causing us to feel uncertain about our financial future.

Market fluctuations can lead people to make poor decisions, such as selling out of fear or investing more out of greed when prices are high. The constant movement and unpredictability of the market make it challenging to stick to a specific investment strategy, even with the discipline of checking regularly.

ABILITY TO LEVERAGE

One of the biggest advantages of real estate is that it can be leveraged. In other words, you can get a mortgage on real estate, which can quadruple your return on investment! Let me explain:

Let's say you buy a rental property for $100,000 in cash. Now, instead of buying the house for cash, you get a mortgage after paying 25 percent (or $25,000) as down payment. By doing so, you could now buy four houses with the same $100,000, thereby increasing your returns by four times with the same amount of starting capital. It's quite difficult to get a loan from a bank to invest in the stock market, which further emphasizes real estate as the better investment option.

PAY LESS: REAL ESTATE HAS INCREDIBLE TAX BENEFITS

Real estate is an attractive investment option not only because it offers a steady stream of passive income but also because it comes with many tax benefits. One of the most significant advantages of investing in real estate is the tax deductions you can take advantage of.

- Property expenses are tax deductible: Tax deductions are a powerful benefit of real estate investing. Property upkeep, maintenance, and interest rates are common expenses associated with owning

real estate. The tax codes allows for a variety of deductions related to these expenses, which can offset your rental income and reduce your tax burden.
- Depreciation: Even though the value of real estate increases over time, the tax code allows real estate investors to claim depreciation of the property as a tax deduction. For tax purposes, depreciation is a way a real estate investor recoups their investment. The depreciation deduction reduces your net taxable income but doesn't impact cash flow.
- 1031 Exchanges: If you sell your property and reinvest the proceeds into a replacement property, there is no immediate tax consequence for that sale. Therefore, the 1031 exchange allows a real estate investor to defer their capital gains taxes associated with the sale.

Moreover, real estate is subject-to lower capital gains tax rates (not taxed at ordinary income rates), and the depreciation expense can allow you to increase your cash flow over time by reporting a lower income, even though the value of the property appreciates.

EFFECTIVE INFLATION HEDGE

GDP growth and the demand for real estate go hand-in-hand. When an economy expands, the demand for property often increases the cost of rent. For that reason, investors see higher capital values.

In essence, real estate maintains a strong buying power of capital because it can pass on a portion of the inflationary pressure to tenants. But at the same time, capital appreciation absorbs another part of the inflationary pressure, which you can't count on with other asset classes. All things considered, real estate investors get tons of benefits. They can build wealth much faster through a combination of passive income, tax advantages, leverage, and stable cash flow.

Are there drawbacks to real estate investing? Of course, there are. Liquidity has always been somewhat of an issue, even in a high-demand market. It can take months to close a real estate deal and turn one of your assets into cash, while stock and bond transactions are completed in seconds. Despite this drawback, real estate is easier to understand and represents a distinct asset class that can improve the risk versus return profile of your portfolio.

Whether on its own or as a way of diversifying your current portfolio, the tax breaks, steady cash flow, and inflation protection are valuable benefits to any type of investor.

WE HAVE A WINNER

Finally, we cross-referenced our own investment goals to what real estate could offer us.

1. BUILDING GENERATIONAL WEALTH

We've heard the saying by famed billionaire Andrew Carnegie that around 90 percent of millionaires made their wealth by investing in real estate. Over 100 years later, today's millionaires still agree.

The day you buy real estate is the day you start building equity. As the value of real estate goes up over the years, so does your wealth. In other words, real estate is an improvable asset. These are tangible assets made of brick and concrete. Through sweat equity or renovations, repairs, and other projects, you can force the appreciation of your asset.

Over time, you can build more equity, and as you do, you also gain more leverage to the point that you can buy more investment properties. Thus, you're able to substantially increase your cash flow and build more wealth.

2. TIME FREEDOM

Investing in real estate, particularly in long-term buy-and-hold rental properties, offers a great way to move away from trading hours for dollars. One of the most attractive reasons to invest in real estate is the cash flow aspect. Generating positive cash flow after making mortgage payments is a great way to create passive income that can build equity replace your nine-to-five job.

As you accumulate more assets over time and hold onto them, you're essentially "asset stacking"—the more assets you own, the higher your cash flow, and the higher your net worth. Passive rentals allowed us to obtain the time freedom we were desired.

3. LOCATION FREEDOM

Our future lifestyle was our North Star, and real estate investing provided us with the flexibility we needed to be present with our kids, exploring playgrounds, or traveling the world whenever we wanted to. In fact, we often buy properties sight unseen while we are traveling overseas.

What is your vision of the future? With a carefully crafted strategy, you can collapse time and start living the life you want sooner rather than later. It all starts with your vision.

CHAPTER THREE

How We Defined Our Real Estate Investing Strategy

When we started investing in real estate, our main objective was to obtain financial freedom. Our aim was not just incremental growth, but exponential growth. Retirement in old age was not our goal; rather, we wanted to retire in five years. After each of us had worked in the corporate sector for fifteen years, we realized that financial freedom would not be an option if we continued sticking to the status quo. Even those who were much older and higher up in our companies were far from achieving financial freedom, and that was a pretty good indicator to us that we needed to find another way.

As Warren Buffett says, "Sometimes, it's not about how hard you row your boat, it's about the boat that you're in." And we had come to realize that we were in the wrong boat.

We connected with seasoned real estate investors who had been investing for a long time, and we saw a pattern. Most of the investors we spoke with said they dabbled in multiple strategies—they did a flip on the side and had a couple of rentals, some held a real estate agent's license, some wholesaled their own deals, and some got a General Contractor's license to save on construction costs. We were a bit taken aback, and we asked them how many hours they worked a week on real estate. The answer was anywhere between forty and sixty hours a week.

For those of you who feel guilty at the thought of not wanting to work long hours, please know, we see you. We both grew up with very strong work ethics and appreciate hard work. We weren't trying to shy away from hard work, but we had already invested a lot of time trying better our kids' lives while also climbing the corporate ladder. Unfortunately, while doing so, we weren't able to spend time as a family, and we weren't able to take care of our own health. This is how the corporate world is structured. This is the reality of today's world. To break free from it, we need to think differently and have the courage to take action. We didn't mind working hard if we needed to, but we wanted to do so on our own terms, based on what mattered the most to us.

We realized that time was a valuable resource, and we were clear that we weren't getting into real estate investing solely to generate more income. Our main goal was to create wealth and time freedom; we didn't want to sign up for yet another nine-to-five job. In order to reach our goals, we realized it was very important to pick one strategy and master it. Rather than growing one inch in twelve directions, we chose to grow twelve inches in one direction. By being hyper-focused on one single strategy, we were able to build a $10 million cash-flowing rental portfolio in five years.

In trying to figure out the best real estate investing strategy, we asked ourselves three key questions.

1. WHAT KIND OF LIFE DO I ENVISION MYSELF LIVING?

We noticed that many people in corporate, including myself, often prioritize their careers over their personal lives. We only started seeing the drawbacks of this once we had kids. We often felt trapped in a life that we had voluntarily chosen. It's no wonder that corporate life is often referred to as 'golden handcuffs' or 'hamster wheel.' Some people do it out of ambition, eager to climb the corporate ladder and achieve success. Others feel the financial benefits of their job were too great to sacrifice, despite the long hours and demanding workload.

The culture of the corporations also plays a role, with a strong emphasis on work ethic and the expectation of being available at all times—even after starting a family. Others simply aren't aware of the impact their job has on their overall well-being.

With time, it has become increasingly clear to us that it is important to always prioritize your lifestyle as you build your life. After all, your career is only one aspect of who you are, and it's crucial to take care of your mental and physical health, relationships, and overall happiness.

This is a realization many high-achieving professionals come to as they advance in their careers, and this is the reason real estate investing can offer them hope. However, we've noticed that many real estate investors end up going from the frying pan to the fire as they develop their portfolio.

We remember when we first started investing in real estate. We were so focused on making it a success that we often found ourselves working long hours. Since we didn't want to compromise time with the kids, we ended up sacrificing sleep and well-being. We believed that putting all our efforts into the business was the key to success, and we were willing to do whatever it took to make it work.

Within just a few weeks, we realized that this approach wasn't sustainable. We weren't taking care of our own well-being. Remembering the reasons why we started investing in real estate in the first place, we immediately started setting boundaries. And you know what? Our business actually improved as a result. With more clarity and focus, we found ourselves working more productively and creatively.

It is possible to be a successful real estate investor and still prioritize your lifestyle. It is possible to have it all: a thriving real estate investing business and a fulfilling life outside of work. That's why we always advise aspiring investors to put their lifestyle first when choosing their strategy and method of execution. It is a decision that pays off in the long run.

Before embarking on any real estate investment, ask yourself, "What kind of life do I envision myself living?"

This seemingly simple question it is very important. This question is the reason why we don't flip properties. We don't wholesale our own deals. We don't DIY our projects. Because lifestyle is the number one priority for us. While we had good incomes from our day jobs, we lacked time for ourselves and our family. Defining the life we wanted was essential in deciding which real estate strategy to pursue.

We figured out that if we flipped properties, the only way we were going to make money was by continuing to flip properties. The day we stopped flipping, our income would stop. If one of us became a real estate agent, we would only earn income when involved in buying or selling properties. If we DIYed our construction projects, we'd be at the jobsite all day.

That's why we decided to invest in real estate. Our goal was to spend more time with my family, and to have time freedom. By prioritizing this question, we were able to discover a unique strategy and approach to the real estate industry. It has allowed us to change status quo. It allowed us to find our calling and help others do the same.

2. WHAT AM I WILLING TO GIVE UP TO GET THE LIFE I WANT?

We all lead very full lives, juggling full-time jobs, marriage, kids, social obligations, and a myriad of errands, leaving us with limited time.

Starting a whole new business, though exciting, can be intimidating and require us to step outside of our comfort zones. To illustrate this, here are a few things we gave up, and we invite you to ask yourself this question, and then follow along to see where you land:

Shiny objects: Real estate investment requires time in the market, effort, and patience to succeed. New investors need to research and evaluate properties, network with vendors and service and professionals, and deal with all the paperwork and legalities involved. As exciting as a new adventure is, there will be times when the process may feel less than thrilling. The real money is made behind the scenes and keeping our heads down with a single strategy until we can implement in our sleep and then again pivoting to scale it further with bigger projects rather than changing strategies again.

Money: Investing in real estate requires SOME capital. It is a myth that no capital is required in real estate and leads lots of new investors to believing that they can achieve financial freedom without investing any of their own money. New investors may need to save up, borrow funds, or liquidate retirement accounts to get started.

Comfort: Any form of investment carries some inherent risks involved. For investors who have little experience taking risks, the process can feel stressful, especially at first. Investors may have to accept uncertainty and setbacks as they learn the ropes and build their portfolios.

Job stability: If an individual decides to become a full-time real estate investor, they may have to sacrifice job stability and benefits like a steady income, health insurance, and paid time off.

Interestingly, it helps to know your "non-negotiables," as giving up the above seems much easier when you know you are not sacrificing your non-negotiables. For us, our non-negotiable was spending time with our kids and family. It was a very visceral need, and we felt it with every fiber of our beings.

Our second non-negotiable was that we didn't want anybody else dictating our potential. We didn't want a boss to be able to decide whether we got a promotion after working hard for two or three years. We wanted to grow on our own terms.

Those were our two non-negotiables, and we realized their value. Once you know your non-negotiables and feel certain about pursuing them, it appears insignificant in comparison to give up other things. As investors who have experienced this firsthand, we can say that no amount of stability and comfort can replace generational wealth and freedom. Neither of us ever regretted giving up our high-paying careers.

Identify your top two to three non-negotiables and be willing to let go of other things in order to achieve the kind of life you want and deserve.

3. WHAT'S MY "WHY"?

Achieving financial freedom is a long-term goal that requires patience, the willingness to make uncomfortable choices (like walking away from a high-paying job), and the ability to navigate failures. To pursue this goal effectively, we needed a clear reason for as to why we were doing so.

For us, financial freedom meant having time, income, and wealth. While we each had our own priorities, there was significant overlap in our desires: We wanted to build generational wealth, create passive income streams, and have the freedom to spend time with loved ones, raise children, and make a positive impact in the world.

We didn't know it when we started, but in hindsight, we hadn't truly understood our true "why." It was only when we dug deeper that we realized what we truly wanted, and this is the "Seven Levels of Why" exercise.

When I (Palak) asked myself why I wanted to go into real estate, financial freedom quickly came up. The "Seven levels of Why" exercise is simple: just continue asking yourself "why?" until you can no longer ask that question. Usually, you get the answer before you ask this question seven times.

So, why did I want financial freedom? Because I wanted to spend more time with my kids.

I continued asking myself why I wanted to spend time with my kids. And after finishing the exercise, I realized that quitting my job and investing in real estate wasn't only about spending time with my kids.

My overarching goal, my real need, was I wanted to leave a legacy, and I wanted to do it on my own terms. I didn't want somebody else controlling how much money I make, whether or not I get time off from work. Just because I'm a parent and want to spend time with my kids, I didn't want to be penalized at work by not getting that promotion.

Find your why. You will need it to build something amazing.

We invite you to do this exercise with us. Ask yourself what your "why" is for reaching financial freedom. When you get an answer, try asking the question again until you can no longer ask that question any longer. Know the depths of what deeply motivates you and make that the driving force behind your actions.

Knowing your why can provide motivation and clarity when working toward financial freedom. It helps you stay focused on your long-term goals and make decisions that align with your values and priorities. When times get tough—and they will when pursuing audacious goals such as financial freedom—your why can serve as a reminder of why you're making sacrifices and help you stay the course. After all, if it was easy, everyone would be doing it. Our "why" has always been our North Star that has guided us and enabled us to make big decisions quickly.

Having a clear why also helps you to prioritize your spending and investments. When you understand what you're working toward, you're less likely to make impulsive decisions that undermine your progress. Instead, you're more likely to make choices that align with your goals, even when they may be uncomfortable in the short term.

Knowing your why also helps you to stay motivated and focused. Financial freedom is a long-term goal that requires sustained effort, and having a clear why can help you stay focused on the bigger picture. When you understand why you're working toward financial freedom, you're more likely to make the right choices and stay committed to your goals, even when they seem out of reach.

In short, knowing your why is essential to creating a successful financial plan and achieving financial freedom. It provides the motivation and clarity you need to stay focused, make good decisions, and work toward your goals with determination and purpose.

We sometimes joke and say we're suffering the side effects of becoming of real estate investors. These, in reality, are the outcomes of asking these three questions and truly changing how we live our lives to fit the audacious financial freedom goals we had and achieved. We have seen these transformations time and again within our community and students, and the results are truly amazing. It goes beyond financial freedom and makes this outcome so much more. Here are some examples.

- Loss of toxic relationships: Once you know you can set audacious objectives and achieve them, you will accept no one but those who truly want the best for you around you.
- Trading Netflix and mindless scrolling for Zillow; this alone will help you find a few extra hours each day.
- Disregard for all shopping, except houses! We're not into Lamborghinis or expensive handbags (not that there's anything wrong with that). Instead, we love focusing on looking for houses to buy. Each property brings investors closer to living the life that they want.

A STRATEGY THAT ALIGNED WITH OUR GOALS

After gaining clarity on our "why," we also needed to zero in on our goals. As you'll see in this chapter, knowing our goals helped us tailor our chosen real estate investment strategy to our specific needs and circumstances.

We wanted our strategy to align with three goals: Generational Wealth, Passive Income, and Time and Location Freedom. We made it our mantra and discussed it extensively, to the point where we started referring to these as our guiding principles.

Many evenings were spent talking about which strategy was right for us. We would study every strategy and assessed whether it fit the three goals we had in mind. After a few weeks, we realized several important things.

A SHIFT IN MINDSET

Wealth, Passive Income, and Freedom were essentially pipe dreams for us as new investors. We had no knowledge or firsthand experience with these three guiding principles. We didn't even know how to think about them, let alone find a strategy that would fit all three.

We knew that to become wealthy, build passive income, and achieve time and location independence, we needed to break the shackles of the mindset that we had been passed down to us, albeit with good intentions, from our previous generations.

Most of our peers who were high earners did not know that a high income did not automatically mean wealth.

We noticed that almost all of the high earners we knew had worked hard to achieve the long-term goal of higher education and climbing the corporate ladder. However, once that was achieved, most prioritized immediate needs over long-term goals. Their minds were more occupied with how they were going to spend the money they earned (and probably save some of it) and behave like consumers, rather than spend time learning how they would build assets and become more future-oriented in order to behave like an investor. They assumed they would retire at the age of sixty or more, and they didn't know they could even have the option to retire early.

We found that changing our mindset was going to be critical to our success, and that memory remains fresh in our minds today as we help new investors who are in need of the same mindset shifts. Most of the investors we have worked with come from highly tactical, scientific, or numbers-oriented professional backgrounds, such as doctors, nurses, lawyers, engineers, and architects. While they excel in their professions, they struggle with the same mindset issues that held us back when we first started. It has become our mission, purpose, and calling to provide the same life-changing mindset shifts to others.

EXECUTING GENERATIONAL WEALTH, PASSIVE INCOME, AND TIME AND LOCATION FREEDOM

When aiming for financial freedom, it's not just about the strategy, it's also about the method of execution. If you take away nothing else from this book, please remember this ONE thing. We see many new investors erroneously focus simply on the strategy. As you dive deeper, it becomes evident that it is not about the strategy itself, it is about how it is executed.

In fact, the method of execution is more important to achieve success in a way that is more aligned with time and location freedom than the strategy itself.

To achieve our goals, we broke down our three guiding principles into smaller steps to make the right decisions.

GENERATIONAL WEALTH

To build generational wealth, focus on three elements:

1. VELOCITY OF MONEY

Most of us aren't born with a silver spoon in our mouths. Typically, we have a finite amount of money to work with. Therefore, we had to figure out how we could increase the velocity of money. By doing our own deals and keeping all the profits, we could build assets quickly by recycling our money from one deal to the next. This approach allowed us to make the most of our limited capital. Investing in other people's deals was out of question for us—a great strategy for diversification if we had additional capital to deploy, but we wanted to invest our finite amount of money into our own deals to get better returns as we started out.

2. USING COMMERCIAL FINANCING AND NOT PEDDLING REAL ESTATE

In order to create generational wealth, it's crucial to own assets for the long term—there's no way around it. This is something that wealthy families know and pass down to their children. You don't create generational wealth by being involved in real estate from a transactional perspective. For example, when you are involved in flipping, wholesaling, or becoming a real estate agent, you create short-term income, but not long-term wealth. Owning assets is what creates generational wealth. So, we eliminated strategies like flipping, wholesaling, or becoming a real estate agent.

Second, to rapidly build wealth through real estate investing, we knew we had to understand and master commercial financing. While conventional financing is acceptable for buying your primary residence, it's challenging to scale a rental portfolio due to its limitations.

3. MASTERMINDS AND COACHES

As the saying goes, "your network is your net worth." A coaching program or mastermind can provide you with the opportunity to network with like-minded people who share the same goals and strategies as you. A community of people who have the same goals will help you through your lows and celebrate your successes. And a coach will help you avoid making mistakes that could have otherwise cost you tens of thousands of dollars. This is crucial for collapsing time and being able to create generational wealth without having to wait for generations to come.

PASSIVE INCOME

After spending years trading our time for money in our nine-to-five jobs, it became essential for us to create assets that would earn passive income.

1. SYSTEMS IN PLACE FOR LANDLORDING

We knew that if we were going to own rental properties, we didn't want to deal with late-night tenant phone calls. So, we would have to put systems in place for landlording, or outsource it to a good property manager.

2. LONG-TERM BUY-AND-HOLDS WITH LOW VOLATILITY

Long-term rentals offer a predictable income on a monthly and yearly basis, with limited volatility. Other strategies like short-term rentals can be highly seasonal and vulnerable to events that affect travel (e.g., COVID-19), and can also be impacted by government regulations. Strategies like medium-term rentals are great, however, they require more involvement than long-term rentals.

3. BUILDING IT LIKE A BUSINESS

Most "mom and pop" investors don't know how to scale because they lack systems, teams, and processes that they would need to expand while also managing their existing portfolio. We recognized that regardless of strategy we chose, we would need to execute it in our own unique way.

TIME AND LOCATION FREEDOM

Of course, as mentioned before, we wanted the freedom to spend time with our family and be able to work from anywhere in the world.

1. BEST PRACTICES IN BUSINESS THAT CAN BE IMPLEMENTED IN REAL ESTATE

Our experience from our corporate backgrounds was in systems, processes, and helping build business departments from scratch, but in we worked in two completely different industries and in different capacities. Coupled with our extensive education through business coaching programs and masterminds, we were able to implement the best practices in business within our venture in real estate investing. This gave birth to a blueprint on how to implement an existing strategy in a way that most real estate investors don't.

2. A BUSINESS THAT CAN BE RUN REMOTELY

We built our business in a way that allows us to grow it from anywhere in the world. The true test of this practice was when we bought seven units (three duplexes and a single-family home) sight unseen while were traveling internationally. All the units were renovated and rented out in a few months, without the need for us to visit the property ourselves. We started looking deeper into what had made this successful and found that a rock star team and effective processes were the key components that drove our business like an engine. Our agent viewed the properties via video conference with us, our contractor rehabbed all the units using a template that he followed for all properties (exact same kitchen, bathroom, flooring, paint, etc.), and our property management company rented out all the units.

These are just a few examples of how you can build a business that scales no matter where you are in the world. We decided to do a deeper dive into strategizing a unique system, and we further distilled our blueprint.

The BRRRR strategy was a clear winner. We met many veteran real estate investors who had been implementing this strategy to scale their portfolio for decades, through many market cycles and changes and had successfully built generational wealth and passive income. BRRRR is what has allowed us to scale fast while minimizing our risks.

Other advantages of BRRRR are as follows:

1) Removes the capital constraint. Increasing the velocity of money allows an investor implementing this strategy to build generational wealth without starting with hundreds of thousands of dollars.
2) Allows an investor to buy properties for cents on the dollar. Buying distressed properties as raw material for this strategy allows an investor to acquire properties at lower than market value.
3) Forces the appreciation instead of waiting for years for a property to appreciate. This strategy allows for instant (relatively speaking) forced appreciation, one of the most significant advantages in real estate investing.

CHAPTER FOUR

Introducing the Scale Framework for BRRRR

Over the last few years, BRRRR has become a buzz word. Chances are you've already heard about it. Let's quickly cover what this strategy means and why it is so powerful.

TRADITIONAL BRRRR

BRRRR is an acronym that stands for:

B: Buy. This entails purchasing a distressed property that can be acquired for less than its market value. They say you make your money in real estate when you buy, and this is especially true in this case. Most buyers do not want a distressed property because of the work that goes along with it. This allows us to purchase it at pennies on the dollar due to lack of competition.

R: Rehab. Once the property is acquired, the next step is to renovate it. This renovation process for the right property allows it to appreciate in value, creating forced and instant equity. One of the greatest wealth builders in real estate is appreciation. Normally, this appreciation happens over many years; however, the BRRRR strategy allows you increase your property's market value in a matter of months.

R: Rent. As they say, cash flow is king. Renting out the property is the next step in this process. This is also known as stabilizing. The difference between the rent and mortgage plus any operating expenses or vacancy will become your passive income, ultimately generating profit.

R: Refinance. Once the property is stabilized and generating income, the property can be refinanced. The advantage of forced appreciation is that now the value of the property is more than the purchase price and rehab cost combined. This number is known as the after=repair value (ARV). A lender would be willing to give you a long-term mortgage for the property, typically at 75–80 percent of the ARV. This allows you to pull out the money you invested in the deal, which can be used to invest in more properties.

R: Repeat. This final step involves repeating the process with another property, using the original funds from the previous deal to invest in the next one. The cycle can continue indefinitely, allowing you to scale your portfolio rapidly and build long-term wealth.

CHALLENGES WITH BRRRR

Implementing BRRRR can come with some challenges, which often results in people giving up or not getting started at all. Let's discuss some common challenges:

LIMITED CAPITAL TO SCALE FAST

For those of us who are not trust fund babies, having to come up with $50,000–$100,000 for the Buy and Rehab phase of the property is difficult. Even though we know will receive the funds back during the Refinance phase, it's still difficult to do multiple projects simultaneously in order to scale. A big question that people have is, "How do I finance this deal if I think it's a good one?"

A BRRRR project takes about six to nine months to complete the cycle. Once you refinance, you can reuse the capital and deploy it for the next project (i.e., Repeat). However, we wanted to do more than one or two projects a year to be able to retire quickly. But we only started with $25,000. So, we had to figure out a way to increase the velocity of money.

LIMITED TIME

Limited time is one of the biggest challenges that investors face when implementing BRRRR. A common question we get is, "I have a full-time job. How do I find time to Buy the property, Rehab it, Rent it out, and Refinance it?"

When we first started, both of us had really demanding corporate careers, a two-year-old and a newborn. And we didn't have much family support because both our parents live half-way across the world in India. Needless to say, we had very limited time.

LACK OF SKILLS

As David Greene says in his book on the subject,[1] BRRRR is like getting

---

[1] *Buy, Rehab, Rent, Refinance, Repeat: The BRRRR Rental Property Investment Strategy Made Simple* by David Greene. Find it at www.biggerpockets.com/brrrrbook.

a black belt in real estate! There are many ways to increase profitability, which means you might feel the need to acquire many skills, like becoming a real estate agent or wholesaling your own deals for the Buy phase, doing your own renovation projects during Rehab phase, etc. So, with a full-time job, it can be intimidating to get started.

We faced this when we first started with BRRRR. We heard in podcasts and blogs that in order to be successful, you need to learn as many skills as possible. For instance, if you get a real estate agent's license, you can earn higher profits on each deal since you will also be the agent for each BRRRR deal. If you DIY your projects, or if you start a construction company, you could earn even more on each deal. Or if you wholesale your own deal, you could maximize the profits. And so on. As professionals who had worked hard to climb the corporate ladder, working on strategy for corporations, it seemed to be counterintuitive advice to scale. We knew there had to be a better way.

LIVING IN AN EXPENSIVE MARKET

About 40 percent of the investors we work with live in an expensive market. The issue with the expensive markets is that the majority are more suitable for a flip than a BRRRR, making it tough for a new investor to identify properties to Buy and even Rehab it from a distance.

DECISION FATIGUE AND OVERWHELM

The BRRRR strategy involves several steps, with what's almost like sub-strategies within the single overarching strategy. This can be further exacerbated by the complexities involved in each step, which may lead to decision fatigue, especially for inexperienced investors. Building any business from scratch in it of itself is tough due to risks, uncertainties, lack of knowledge, skills, experience, and network. Combine that with building a business that is as complex as BRRRR with its sub-strategies within it, and it can feel overwhelming.

SCALE FRAMEWORK

As we began executing our first BRRRR, we ran into every one of these challenges listed above! So we focused on building a blueprint for executing the BRRRR strategy that was in alignment with our three guiding principles, which are:

- Create Generational Wealth

- Generate Passive Income
- Create Time and Location Freedom

Time and Location freedom was particularly important to us. Using these guiding principles, we created the SCALE framework for the BRRRR strategy. Over the past few years, we've acquired millions of dollars in real estate using the SCALE framework and have also helped hundreds of other investors all over the United States do the same. So, we know that this strategy works!

In this book, we will share our blueprint, the SCALE framework. Here is what we will cover:

S: Scalable Acquisitions and Deal Analysis (a.k.a. Buy)
In this chapter, we explain how to find a city and neighborhood to implement the BRRRR strategy in a scalable way, defining your ideal property avatar to save time by only analyzing deals that fit your strategy. In addition, we will also go over how to analyze deals accurately, building a deal machine. We'll also cover how to build other systems, processes, and teams such as the Location Freedom Framework, so you can acquire properties from anywhere in the world.

C: Construction that Scales (a.k.a. Rehab)
In this chapter, we will teach you how to estimate your rehab budget accurately using the 3-phase framework, the Goldilocks principle when identifying condition of a property, rehabbing your property so that is aligned with key stakeholders, using the 3-T framework to manage your rehab projects. Additionally, we will explain how to use systems, processes, and teams to manage your rehab, even if you are investing out of state.

A: Adding Cash Flow (a.k.a. Rent)
Here, we will not only explain how to rent the property but also how you can maximize your cash flow as your scale your portfolio, without having to answer any late-night tenant phone calls. We will also get into some of our software, systems, and tools such as the tenant acquisition funnel and virtual showings.

L: Leverage and Commercial Financing (a.k.a. Refinance)
In this chapter, we will explain how to scaling exponentially by two key elements. First, we will discuss up-front leverage to purchase and rehab

the property, which is critical to solving the issue of limited capital. Second, we will cover unlocking the growth potential of a portfolio using commercial finance for stabilized properties. In addition, we will discuss systems, processes, and teams to effectively scale.

E: Exponential Growth (a.k.a. Repeat)
Throughout the SCALE framework, we will show you how to implement BRRRR in a scalable manner. In this chapter, we will introduce additional frameworks that will help you effectively prioritize and manage your most critical resource: time. We will cover tactics to implement the 80/20 rule, creating a bank of Standard Operating Procedures, offer advice on hiring and managing a team, and scaling with small multifamily properties.

CHAPTER FIVE

Scalable Acquisitions and Deal Analysis (a.k.a. Buy)

The goal of the Buy phase in the BRRRR strategy is to buy a distressed property that is under market value.

We supercharged the Buy process with Scalable Acquisitions, which has four components:

1. Identifying your neighborhood
2. Identifying your ideal property avatar
3. Analyzing deals accurately
4. Offer to close

1. IDENTIFYING YOUR NEIGHBORHOOD

When we identify a market to invest in, we look at the following factors:

POPULATION IN THE CITY IS INCREASING

One of the key indicators of a developing city is its population growth over the past few years. An increase in population suggests a net positive migration into the city, which in turn leads to more demand for housing. This leads to more economic growth, which leads to population growth, further fueling the demand for housing.

To assess population growth, visit www.city-data.com and look at the population stats over the last ten years. If the population has increased, that is a positive sign. If the population has decreased, that is a sign that people are moving away from the city, and home prices are likely to decrease in the future. We like to look at trends over a longer period of time, which is why we examine the past ten years, because that is a long enough timeframe to provide a reliable picture. Some people may only consider population migration trends for the past two years, but this is a relatively short timeframe, and the trend could reverse.

THERE IS A DIVERSITY OF EMPLOYERS

In combination with increasing population, we also like to see diversity of employers in a city. What do we mean by diversity of employers? Ideally, you want to invest in a city which has employers in different industries. For example, if a city is only reliant on tourism, it would be at risk in case the tourism industry gets disrupted (like it did during the COVID-19 pandemic). If a city is a university town and solely relies on students for rentals, what happens if the university shuts down?

That is why we prefer to see and invest in diverse industries. For instance, we decided to invest in Philadelphia, PA, because it has a large health care industry, several big universities, corporate employers, among other industries.

DEVELOPMENT IS HAPPENING IN THE NEIGHBORHOOD

Is there noticeable development happening in the neighborhood? We invest in areas that have a lot of investor activity—lots of flips happening, construction projects, and the like. An easy way to identify neighborhood development is by looking in Zillow (or any other app you may use like Redfin). Pull up the neighborhood or zip code you're interested in and review homes listed for sale as well as recently sold homes.

You would want to look at this neighborhood in two ways.

1. Is there a sufficient inventory of distressed properties? Ideally, there should at least be four or five such properties for sale in the zip code. These are the kind of properties you will acquire for BRRRR.
2. Are some of the homes recently renovated? If so, that is a sign that development is happening in the neighborhood. Look at the homes up for rent in Zillow in your neighborhood. If you see homes that are recently renovated that are being rented out, that is also a sign that development is happening in the neighborhood. These renovated properties are the ones you will use as "comps" when estimating your after-repair value (we will go into this in more detail later in the book).

THE 1 PERCENT RULE

For investments properties, including BRRRR properties, it's important that they generate positive cash flow each month. If your monthly rent doesn't cover the PITI (Principle, Interest, Taxes, and Insurance) at the very least, the property won't cash flow. And it is difficult to scale with properties that lose money each month!

The 1 percent rule is an easy way to determine whether a property will cash flow. This rule measures the price of an investment property against the gross income it will generate. For example, if my property is valued at $150,000, and it can generate $1,500 a month in rent, it meets the 1 percent rule.

Because $150,000 x 1% = $1,500 in monthly rent

Now, consider an example of a property that doesn't meet the 1 percent rule. Let's say the value of the property is $500,000, and it rents for $2,500 a month.

$500,000 x 1% = $5,000 in monthly rent

Since this property earns significantly less monthly rent than $5,000, it would be tough to generate positive monthly cash flow.

Now, 1 percent is more a rule of thumb than an accurate calculation. You should still do more detailed deal analysis (covered later in this chapter), to make sure the deal actually works for BRRRR. However, the rule can be used to see if a neighborhood would work for BRRRR.

For example, if majority of the single-family homes in a neighborhood are priced at $350,000 or above, and the monthly rents for those properties are only around $1,800, chances are you won't cash flow.

The neighborhoods we invest in typically have property values from around $100,000 up to $250,000.

2. IDENTIFYING YOUR IDEAL PROPERTY AVATAR

Having a property avatar allows you focus on deals that meet your criteria and quickly eliminate the ones that don't. When you are starting out with BRRRR, it is best to keep it simple.

You can follow the rule of three Ss for your property avatar—Small, Simple, and Scalable. Although we discuss this later in the book, we wanted to share here because it's relevant.

Small: Start with something small. For example, a three-bed/one-bath single-family row home in the city or a small ranch in the suburbs. A smaller investment is a great playground for a new investor. It allows you to learn from your mistakes while limiting your risk. Figuring out how to find a BRRRR-able property is like riding a bike, and it's much easier to learn how to ride a balance bike first.

Simple: We get emails every day from new investors who are just starting out. They want to know how to negotiate a FSBO (for sale by owner), or how to buy a property with a cloudy title, etc. Going after a needle in a haystack deal makes it difficult to scale. There are plenty of deals on the Multiple Listing Service (MLS) and off-market deals that wholesalers can bring to you.

Scalable: For your property avatar, pick a type of property that is abundantly available in your neighborhood. For example, in the neighborhoods we invest in, most single-family homes are three-bedroom/one-bathroom townhomes with an unfinished basement. Picking this profile as our property avatar gives us access to majority of homes on the market.

Although Property Avatars may vary by location, here is a template that works well in most neighborhoods:

1) Three-bedroom/one-bathroom single-family home
2) Between 800 sq. ft. and 1,500 sq. ft. (properties smaller than 800 sq. ft. are often difficult to rent)
3) The house needs renovation (typically outdated kitchen and bathrooms at a minimum). We'll cover the condition and rehab in more detail later in the book.

SINGLE-FAMILY VERSUS CONDOMINIUMS

We often get asked if it's possible to BRRRR a condominium. Here are some reasons why we don't recommend investing in condominiums for the BRRRR strategy (or in general for buy and hold rentals):

- HOA Fees: Condominiums typically come with Homeowner Association (HOA) fees that can increase the overall cost of ownership and reduce the cash flow potential of the investment. HOA fees typically increase over time.
- Restrictions: HOA may have more restrictions on the ability to rent out the condominium, which has direct negative impact on your ROI.
- Property Management: At times, HOA may handle many of the property management tasks, such as maintenance and repairs, which can limit the control that investors have over the property and its management.

RISK MANAGEMENT

If this is your first BRRRR project, your goal should be to minimize risk. We generally advise new investors to start with properties that have a more predictable rehab process, allowing you to gain experience and knowledge before tackling more challenging projects. Here are some suggestions of properties to avoid for your first project:

- Avoid properties with major fire damage because they can come with a host of hidden and unexpected repair costs. Assessing the full scope of extensive fire damage can be challenging, and budgeting a renovation for such damage can be difficult. Additionally, fire damaged properties may have safety issues or code violations.
- Avoid properties that need major structural rehab, as structural issues can be costly to repair and require significant expertise to address properly. You will likely need to hire a structural engineer, and depending on the extent of structural damage, this can pose significant safety risk if not addressed correctly.
- Avoid properties with severe mold because mold remediation can be a complex and expensive process. Mold can cause health issues and property damage, and it can be challenging to completely eliminate mold without professional remediation. Mold can also be a symptom of underlying structural or moisture issues, which can be difficult to assess.
- Avoid properties with title issues, liens, licensing/zoning problems, as these can lead to significant legal and financial challenges. Title issues or liens on the property can create uncertainty about ownership, making it difficult to refinance the property. Licensing and zoning problems can create legal violations and regulatory issues, potentially resulting in fines and penalties.
- Avoid buying properties that are occupied by tenants. It can be challenging and even unsafe to renovate the property while a tenant is living there. You will need to give the tenant a notice to vacate, and it may take a couple of months or more for the tenant to find another rental. This will delay your project and lead to increased costs. We advise new investors to start with properties that are vacant, or can be delivered vacant upon closing, allowing you to have greater control over the renovation process and avoid the added complexity of dealing with inherited tenants.

You can take on the above projects when you have a couple of rehab projects under your belt.

3. ANALYZING DEALS ACCURATELY

Deal analysis is a critical component of the BRRRR strategy and can help investors make informed decisions about which properties to pursue and how to structure their investments for maximum profitability and success.

By analyzing deals correctly, you can not only identify profitable opportunities but also gain clarity on the right purchase price for the property. This is crucial for achieving success in your BRRRR projects.

THE CASH-OUT/CASH-FLOW TANGO

Cash-out and cash flow are key financial metrics used to evaluate the profitability of an investment property for our strategy.

Cash-out refers to the amount of money an investor can borrow against the value of the property after it has been renovated and increased in value. The goal is to use the cash-out refinance to pay off the initial loan used to purchase the property and cover the renovation costs, allowing the investor to easily recoup their initial investment and continue to hold the property, with no money out of pocket, while also retaining a portion of the equity in the property.

Cash flow, on the other hand, refers to the net income generated by the property after all expenses are accounted for. In our strategy, the goal is to have positive cash flow from the rental income, which can be used to cover ongoing expenses and provide a source of passive income for the investor.

To know whether a deal is worth investing in or not, there are two essential questions to ask:

1. **Will I cash-out?** You need to know if you'll be able to pull all (or most) of your seed money from the deal so that you can invest it in the next deal.
2. **Will I cash flow?** Determine if you'll make a profit each month after paying your mortgage and expenses.

We call this the Cash-Out/Cash-Flow Tango. When you're in growth phase and are focusing on scaling your portfolio, it is best to maximize cash-out. By doing so, you will be able to recycle your cash to buy more properties.

Before we talk in more detail about cash-out and cash flow, let's review some commonly used real estate terms:

KEY TERMS AND ACRONYMS

Cash-Out Terms
- **After-Repair Value (ARV):** After-repair value is the projected market value of the property after you have rehabbed it.
- **Rehab Costs:** The cost to renovate the property (including all materials and labor costs).

- **Soft Costs:** The cost of doing a real estate transaction, including closing costs, holding costs, transfer taxes, insurance, etc.
- **Equity Created:** The forced appreciation that you created by rehabbing the property. This is the magic of BRRRR!
- **Loan-to-Value (LTV):** The loan amount compared to the market value of the property (for example, if you have a loan of $80,000, and your property is worth $100,000, then your LTV is 80 percent).

Cash Flow Terms

- **Rent:** The expected rent for your property.
- **PITI (Principle, Interest, Taxes, and Insurance):** This refers to your monthly mortgage payment after you have refinanced the property into a long-term mortgage.
- **OpEx, CapEx, and Vacancy Reserves:** These are reserves you should set aside each month toward any big-ticket CapEx items (e.g., roof, windows, HVAC), smaller OpEx maintenance items, and for potential vacancy in your property.

Now that you know the terminology, let's look at how you would analyze a deal.

SAMPLE DEAL ANALYSIS

Let's analyze a sample deal. It is a three-bedroom/one-bathroom single-family house located in Philadelphia.

List Price: $80,000
Estimated Rehab Cost: $50,000
Estimated ARV: $200,000
Soft Costs (assuming 10 percent of ARV): $20,000
Estimated Rent: $1,700
Estimated PITI: $1,100

In order to determine whether this is a good deal, we will need to answer the two questions: Will I cash-out, and will I cash flow?

WILL I CASH-OUT?

Let's work backward from the after-repair value (ARV).

The estimated ARV for the property is $200,000. When we refinance the property with a long-term mortgage, we are likely to get an LTV of 75 percent.

Seventy-five percent of $200,000 is $150,000. This means that the bank will give us a long-term mortgage of $150,000 for the property.

Now, in order to pull all of our cash out, our total investment in the property (including purchase price, rehab costs, and soft/other costs), will need to be at or below $150,000.

Let's find out if that's the case.

Our estimated rehab cost is $50,000, and estimated soft costs are $20,000. If we purchase the property for the list price of $80,000, our total investment in the property will be:

$80,000 + $50,000 + $20,000 = $150,000

This means that when we refinance this property with a long-term mortgage, we should be able to pull out our entire investment of $150,000!

The cash-out works! But we still need to determine whether the cash flow works.

WILL I CASH FLOW?

Let's say the estimated rent for the property is $1,700. And let's assume that the monthly PITI once you refinance the property with a long-term mortgage is $1,100.

Rent – PITI = $600 a month

Is $600 your monthly cash flow?

Not quite. We always like to be conservative and account for the following:

Potential Capital and Operational Expenditures (15 Percent of Rent): We like to set aside 15 percent of rent each month for potential expenditures that can arise in the property. We set this amount aside each month in a separate "Reserves" bank account. This is a great way to cover for unexpected expenses that may be incurred in the future.

Potential Vacancy (5 percent of Rent): We also like to set aside 5 percent of rent each month to cover for potential vacancy. Vacancy can occur when a tenant moves out and you are making repairs and cleaning the house, and it also accounts for the time it takes to market the house to potential renters.

So, for this property, CapEx/OpEx (15 percent of rent) is $255, and monthly vacancy (5 percent of rent) is $85.

Therefore, the monthly cash flow is calculated as follows:

Rent – PITI – CapEx/OpEx – Vacancy = Monthly Cash Flow
$1,700 – $1,100 – $255 – $85 = $260

So, with a monthly cash flow of $260, this deal certainly works!

And since both cash-out and cash flow work for this deal, we should acquire this deal. In fact, these numbers refer to one of the deals we did recently!

4. OFFER TO CLOSE

The simple truth behind landing the best deals is skill in offer and negotiation. Most new investors we speak with who are professionals in another line of work who aim to scale their portfolio and make work optional are just one single mindset shift away from leveraging their lack of time and steady paycheck to beat full-time investors at this game. This simple truth will set you free, so to speak! and guess what? Even when you do become a full-time investor, this truth will still be the way you run your business and maintain a competitive edge in the market.

There are three main ways to improve your chances of getting a property under contract. As a professional trying to build and scale a real estate portfolio on the side, you will want to simplify this to its bare bones, and the fog will lift. It becomes easier to understand why certain investors get deals consistently while others are unable to succeed despite their best efforts.

1. **Be the First:** In a competitive market or in a slam-dunk deal, there may be multiple offers. To give yourself a competitive edge, build a process that allows you to quickly analyze a deal, get a rehab budget, and put in an offer. For example, if it takes you two days to analyze a deal and a week to put in an offer, chances are, you will lose the deal. Whereas if you can speed up the process and put in an offer within twenty-four hours of a property coming on the market, you will be able to close a lot more deals.
2. **Be the Highest:** Conversations around getting a deal for the lowest possible price can sometimes lead an investor to lose sight of the purpose. If the numbers work, don't hesitate to go higher in price. If you are competing with full-time investors who have no problem being the first, don't be afraid to be willing to pay a few thousand dollars more on a deal to get a competitive edge. If a full-time investor has time on their side, you, on the other hand, still have a steady paycheck. Understand your competitive edge and leverage it to succeed in this game. To clarify, we do not mean you should pay more than what the property is worth. We are simply trying to explain that trying to play by the rules that don't apply to you will not help you succeed, but making your own rules will.
3. **Offer Them the Best Terms:** The third way to get a deal is understand what the seller is looking for and offer it to them if it means no additional time or money on your part. Rely on your team to find these answers and see where you can gain traction. Here are some examples:

a. Would the seller be happier with a cash offer? Many sellers of distressed properties prefer cash because they may be in a bad place financially. Others do not want to rely on mortgage companies declining the loan because the property might not be livable.
   b. Do they want a quick close?
   c. Do they need help getting the property's content out?
   d. Would it be helpful if you made them feel more comfortable by offering a higher earnest money deposit? Be sure to make sure the agreement of sale is worded appropriately so you don't lose the high deposit in case things go south.

Some additional tips you can leverage to get a property under contract are:

- **Escalation Clause:** An escalation clause is a provision in a real estate purchase agreement that allows a buyer to increase their initial offer in the event of a competing offer. The escalation clause specifies a specific amount or percentage by which the buyer is willing to increase their offer above any competing offer, up to a stated maximum price. As a real estate investor, you can leverage an escalation clause to make your offers more competitive and increase your chances of getting a deal under contract.
- **Working Directly with the Listing Agent:** In a competitive market, don't be afraid to use a listing agent as your agent to submit an offer. We find that new investors benefit from this strategy immensely and we highly recommend it. The only exception is if your buyer's agent has already shown you the property, it is unethical to go around them and work with the listing agent. In this industry, or any business for that matter, your reputation is everything. Do not compromise your reputation to get a deal.
- **Leverage Hard Money if You Can't Get a Cash Offer:** Sellers who are looking for a cash offer or a fast close will often accept hard money financing. This is because most hard money lenders can close a deal fairly quickly, sometimes in less than fourteen days. We will cover hard money in detail later in the book.

DUE DILIGENCE

Once you successfully secured the property under contract, the next phase is due diligence. Most investors overlook this step, but it is essential.

Proper due diligence will enable you to vet the deal even further and potentially even re-negotiate the purchase price.

As part of due diligence, there are a few key steps:

1) **Check the Property Title:** Work with an experienced title company to conduct a title search to ensure that there are no liens, judgments, or other encumbrances on the property. Review property tax records to confirm that there are no delinquent taxes or other outstanding obligations.
2) **Check Zoning and Permits:** Verify that the property is zoned for its intended use, and check for any required permits or licenses. Ensure that the property complies with local building codes and regulations. Leverage your agent to make sure there are no issues here.
3) **Firm Up your Rehab Budget:** Later in this book, we will go over the three steps of firming up your rehab numbers, but for now, keep in mind that during diligence, you should hire a home inspection company to inspect the property with a fine-toothed comb. This way you will be able to identify any key renovations that are needed. You could also leverage the home inspection report to re-negotiate the purchase price with the seller.
4) **Obtain Short-Term Financing:** Your short-term lender will be your big brother/sister in providing a sanity check for the numbers that you have in mind for your deal. Obtaining approval from a short-term lender during this phase verifies that a deal is in fact good. Short-term lenders see hundreds of deals on a regular basis and are experienced enough to know when the numbers don't make sense. We will go over this in detail later in the book.

CLOSING

Here are some tips for closing day:

- **Review Closing Documents:** Review the closing documents carefully to ensure that they're accurate and that you understand the terms. Ask questions if anything is unclear.
- **Bring Identification:** Bring proper identification, such as a driver's license or passport, to the closing to verify your identity.
- **Verify Financing:** Ensure that you have the necessary funds and that your lender is prepared to complete the transaction, including closing costs and any required down payment. Verify with the title company or closing attorney how you should bring the funds.

- **Do a Final Walkthrough:** Before the closing, have your agent do a final walkthrough of the property to ensure that it's in the condition that was agreed upon in the purchase contract.
- **Sign the Closing Documents:** Sign the closing documents in the presence of a notary or other authorized representative. Be sure to sign all documents carefully and accurately.
- **Keep Copies of the Documents:** Keep copies of all closing documents for your records. This can include the purchase agreement, closing statement, and any other related documents.
- **Celebrate:** Finally, take a moment to celebrate your new investment and achievement as a real estate investor. This is a significant milestone and deserves recognition.

SYSTEMS AND PROCESSES FOR SCALING

1. BUILDING A DEAL MACHINE

Building a "deal machine" is a critical component of scaling a real estate portfolio using the SCALE blueprint. A deal machine is essential for achieving scalability in real estate investing. By building a repeatable and reliable system for generating new investment opportunities, investors can rapidly scale their portfolio and achieve their investment goals much more quickly.

The following funnel is a visual representation of the various stages involved in the deal machine for acquiring a new real estate investment opportunity.

Deal Machine

The specific steps involved in a deal machine can vary depending on your specific approach, but generally, a deal machine will include several key stages, including:

1. **Lead Generation for Your Property Avatar:** The first stage in a deal machine is lead generation, which involves identifying potential properties that fit your property avatar criteria. This can involve networking with real estate professionals such as agents and wholesalers, building an online presence and social media presence, etc.
2. **Deal Analysis:** The next stage is deal analysis, which involves evaluating the property to determine whether it's profitable.
3. **Negotiation:** Once a property has been identified and qualified, the next stage is negotiation, which involves negotiating the purchase price, terms, and other details of the investment.
4. **Acquisition:** After the terms of the deal have been negotiated, the next stage is acquisition, which involves finalizing the purchase and taking ownership of the property.

The deal machine is shaped like a funnel because it represents the process of filtering a large number of potential properties down to a smaller number of high-quality and scalable opportunities. At the top of the funnel, there are many potential options, which have not yet been qualified or vetted for their potential to cash-out and a cash flow. As the opportunities progress through the various stages of the deal machine, they are filtered. As a result, only a small number of high-quality investment opportunities make it through to the bottom of the funnel, where they are ultimately acquired, renovated, and monetized.

By visualizing the deal process as a funnel, you can better understand the filtering process and the importance of each stage. This can help you identify potential bottlenecks or areas where the deal flow may slow down and make adjustments to ensure efficient and effective identification and acquisition of the best investment opportunities. Overall, the funnel shape of the deal process is a visual representation of the filtering process and the importance of each stage in achieving success and profitability in real estate investing.

For instance, if you've been trying to get a property under contract for months, but can't figure out why, start tracking the numbers in your deal machine. You'll soon figure out where majority of your deals are dropping off. If you're finding that your deals are getting lost around the deal analysis stage, chances are either you are looking in the wrong neighborhood where the strategy does not work or you are being too conservative with your numbers. If your deals are dropping off during the negotiation period, chance are you are either not moving fast enough or there is a disconnect between the market and your expectations of the deal. Let the numbers show you where you are lacking and where your deal machine needs work.

SIMPLIFY TO AMPLIFY

We're here to show investors who have a nine-to-five job how they can succeed at real estate investing despite their existing commitments. One of the biggest ways to succeed as a part-time investor is the "Simplify to Amplify" strategy.

By simplifying your neighborhood and property avatar, you can quickly scan through deals that don't fit your criteria and eliminate them within minutes. Simplification is your superpower here. The biggest impact in scaling this business is through simplification. This will allow you to amplify your efforts without spending all of your time on your efforts and burning out.

2. BUILDING A TEAM/SOURCES OF LEAD GENERATION

Building a team is a critical component of the SCALE framework. Each member of the team plays the role of a source of lead generation for the deal machine. There are many different team members that investors may work with when pursuing BRRRR deals, but three of the most important are agents, wholesalers, and REO specialists. Here's a breakdown of how each of these team members can help you get a BRRRR deal under contract:

REAL ESTATE AGENTS

Real estate agents are licensed professionals who specialize in buying and selling real estate. They have access to the Multiple Listing Service (MLS), which is a database of properties for sale only available to licensed agents. A good agent can help you identify potential opportunities, evaluate the financials of each property, and negotiate the purchase price and terms of the deal. They can also help you navigate the complex process of acquiring a property and ensure that all of the necessary paperwork is completed correctly and on time.

If you are using a real estate agent to check out properties, remember that no one gets paid unless you close. Until you close on a deal (and the commission on distressed properties is low), be respectful of the agent's time and create a long-term relationship.

When you don't close on a deal, let your agent know why. It helps them to understand why you are not interested in a particular deal so they can assist you more effectively in the future.

WHOLESALERS

Wholesalers specialize in finding and acquiring distressed properties and then selling them to other investors at a discount. They typically have a network of contacts in the real estate industry and are often able to find deals that are not available through traditional channels. A good wholesaler can help you identify potential investment opportunities that may not be available to the general public, negotiate the purchase price and terms of the deal, and provide valuable insight into the local real estate market. Local Facebook groups are a great resource to connect with wholesalers and get on their email list. You will identify the big players after watching a Facebook group for a while and noticing who posts the most deals and gets the most comments. Keep in mind, though, that the wholesaling industry is largely unregulated, and make sure you vet the wholesaler by inquiring with other investors in your network and by asking for references. If you don't feel comfortable with any paperwork, do not be afraid to retain an attorney to look it over for you. Similar to working with agents, if you do not move forward on a deal with a wholesaler after analysis and conversations, it is important to help them understand why. It helps them bring other deals that fit your needs in future and creates a long-term relationship.

REO SPECIALISTS

REO (Real Estate Owned) specialists are real estate professionals who specialize in buying and selling properties that have been foreclosed on by the bank. REO specialists have been our superpower in finding deals. They typically have access to a large inventory of distressed properties and can help you identify potential investment opportunities that are available at a significant discount. A good REO specialist can help you navigate the complex process of acquiring a foreclosed property, negotiate the purchase price and terms of the deal, and provide valuable insights into the local real estate market.

3. LOCATION-FREEDOM FRAMEWORK

To scale the Buy process as a BRRRR investor, it is necessary to put a framework in place that allows you to streamline the process of identifying, evaluating, and acquiring distressed properties. By implementing this framework, you can make the process of acquiring new properties more efficient and effective, helping you scale your portfolio fast, while also providing you with location freedom. That way, you can be anywhere in the world, and your acquisition process will continue without interruption.

IDENTIFY

Using the deal machine framework, we get fifty to one hundred deals each week in our inbox. This includes properties on MLS, as well as off-market deals through wholesalers. Having great connections with agents and wholesalers, and being very specific with them about your property avatar, will ensure that you have enough deals to analyze.

EVALUATE

When we talk to new investors, their biggest hurdle is evaluating deals out-of-state, sight unseen. There are several steps to this process to make it more efficient.

Leverage technology: Use technology to your advantage by utilizing software like Zoom, Skype, WhatsApp, or Facetime for virtual tours of the property with your agent.

Leverage processes: Create a simple process detailing what pictures you would like them to provide when at the jobsite. For example, we ask our real estate agent to take videos of the interior, exterior, and the street. We ask the agent to then take pictures of the interior including any labels on mechanicals, any leaks/cracks, and anything else they may find useful. Build a Google form that allows your agent to input all the above information you require for deal analysis, and a Google Drive folder where they can upload pictures and videos.

Leverage skills: To analyze a deal, you need to be as accurate as possible when (a) estimating ARV, (b) estimating rents, and (c) estimating rehab budget. You can leverage your agent's local knowledge to help with estimating the ARV, as well as estimating rents. Agents can also recommend local contractors to get a rehab estimate—we'll cover the rehab budgeting process later in the book.

ACQUIRE

Often, we are asked how we are able to manage the closing process of multiple deals at the same time without stress. The answer? We are extremely organized.

Virtual Assistant: As you scale your portfolio, consider hiring a virtual assistant who can follow an SOP (standard operating procedure) for your process to go from due diligence phase to closing. This could include researching property tax records, working with a title company, vetting and hiring contractors to give you a construction budget, providing documentation to lenders as needed, getting insurance for the property, and managing all the dates outlined in the Agreement of Sale. A well-trained virtual assistant can be your super-power when you are on an acquisition-spree.

Traveling Notaries: We advise all out-of-state investors to look into traveling notaries. This can allow you to close on your deal from the comfort of your home. Traveling notaries can often accommodate a range of scheduling needs, including after-hours or weekend appointments, which can be particularly useful for working professionals who may not be able to take time off during regular business hours. Notaries are required to ensure that the documents are signed correctly, legally, and confidentially.

SYSTEMS

In the context of the BRRRR strategy, a system refers to a set of processes and tools that are used to automate or streamline certain aspects of the real estate investment process. Some examples of systems that can be put in place for the "Buy" step include:

Lead Management System: This type of system helps investors track and organize their leads, allowing them to prioritize their efforts and follow up with leads in a timely manner.

Property Analysis Spreadsheet: Tools such as spreadsheets can help investors quickly and accurately evaluate potential properties and determine if they fit the criteria for the BRRRR strategy. Using a consistent method of analyzing deals will help ensure that you are taking into account all the key criteria.

Closing Management System: This type of system can help streamline the closing process by automating tasks such as document preparation and signature collection.

MEET ROCKSTAR INVESTOR RUPA

When Rupa first became interested in real estate investing, she contacted an agent who then started showing her beautiful condominium properties in A-class (top tier) neighborhoods. The condominiums were great but came with hefty HOA dues and rental restrictions, leaving a rental income that didn't cover the PITI combined with the HOA fees. In theory, the investment looked great because it was a good neighborhood that Rupa was familiar with. However, the numbers didn't make sense. Rupa knew something wasn't right, but she didn't know what was wrong.

You see, Rupa wasn't being shown liabilities rather than cash-flowing assets. These properties could end up taking up more money on a monthly basis than the rent i.e., revenue. We see this often with high earners who live in A-class neighborhoods and work with agents who are familiar with A-class neighborhoods. While these properties may seem like a good way to invest money, they can end up costing more than the rent they generate on a monthly basis. These kinds of properties are not a suitable option for building a scalable rental portfolio that can eventually provide her with financial independence.

With the help of this framework, Rupa has now crossed a multi-million-dollar portfolio which are all cash-flowing assets. In her first year, she purchased six properties!

In the next chapters, we'll walk you through the other components of the BRRRR strategy. Next up is rehab.

CHAPTER SIX
Construction that Scales (Rehab)

Rehabbing is where the magic happens! By renovating the property, you can force the appreciation that would otherwise take years to achieve.

Whether you're a seasoned investor looking to scale your portfolio or a new investor just starting out, rehabbing a property can be an essential tool in achieving your financial goals. Understanding how to renovate properties at scale can be helpful in any real estate investing strategy.

In this chapter, we will dive deep into the rehab process. We will discuss the challenges of rehab and share our step-by-step framework for budgeting a rehab project, determining how much to renovate in order to get the appraisal you want, building your team, managing the rehab process efficiently, and implementing systems and processes to help you scale.

BUDGETING

ESTIMATING YOUR REHAB BUDGET

Estimating your rehab budget correctly is a critical component of the BRRRR strategy. For our first couple of rehab projects, we made the mistake of over-rehabbing the properties. We rehabbed our property as if we were going to flip the property rather than renovate it like a rental. This meant that we were left with more money in the deal than we would have liked.

CHALLENGES

There are many challenges that new investors face when trying to accurately estimate a rehab budget.

Underestimating Costs: Some new investors lack experience in the real estate industry and may not fully understand the costs involved in a rehab project. This can lead to underestimating and having an insufficient budget to work with, which can potentially lead to incorrect deal analysis and buying the wrong property.

Lack of Knowledge: New investors may lack knowledge about the rehab process, including how to assess a property, determine necessary rehab needed, and estimate costs accurately.

Difficulty Finding a Reliable Resource for Budgeting: As we discussed in the section on the deal machine, you may need to look at multiple properties before finding one to make an offer on. New investors often struggle to find a contractor willing to provide budgets for multiple properties without having done business with them before. This can make it challenging to complete projects on time and within budget, as well as delay the process of making an offer on a good deal.

THREE PHASES OF REHAB BUDGETING

To address the challenges mentioned above, we have developed a three-stage framework to estimate your rehab budget, based on where you are in your buying process. Dividing the rehab estimation into three phases allows you to proceed with more confidence into the project.

There are two important things to note:

- With each iteration of the rehab estimate, you increase your accuracy.
- These occur in three different stages of the buying process.

Below are the three phases we use in our rehab estimation framework:

1. Rough estimate prior to placing an offer
2. Tightening numbers during due diligence
3. Final quote and scope of work after closing, but before paying contractor a deposit

Three Phases of Rehab Budgeting
Phases of Rehab Numbers

Eventually, this will become seamless (same contractor)!

So, how do these phases work?

PHASE 1: ESTIMATE

New investors or seasoned investors venturing in a new market may not have established relationships with reliable contractors and vendors, which can make it difficult to obtain quotes quickly and accurately. It may take time to build these relationships and find trusted professionals who can provide reliable estimates. Success loves speed, and good deals go fast. This time is valuable, and this phase allows you to quickly move forward with your numbers to accurately identify a deal that is viable.

In this phase, focus on getting a rough estimate. This will allow you to rapidly put an offer on the property, which will put you in a better position to acquire lucrative deals.

In order to get a rough estimate, you will need to find a contractor who can visit the property and give you a high-level estimate. For example, if the property needs a new kitchen, new bathroom, new flooring, new roof, and some electric needs to be replaced, the contractor should be able to tell you the approximate cost. Be sure to explain to your contractor that this is a rental and not a flip. That way, you won't over-rehab the property. You should add a 10 to 15 percent contingency to this number to be on the safe side.

Once you have this rough estimate, you can do your analysis and see if the cash-out and cash flow numbers work. If they do, then you are ready to put in an offer on the property.

PHASE 2: SOLIDIFY

Congratulations for getting your property under contract! Ideally, new investors should have a due diligence contingency in their offer. That way, you have a few days to perform due diligence and potentially back out of the deal if there are any surprises. Your next step is going to be tightening you your rehab numbers.

To conduct due diligence from a rehab standpoint during the due diligence phase, conduct a thorough inspection of the property to identify any major issues that need to be addressed. We highly recommend hiring a professional home inspector to ensure that all areas of the property are evaluated. Create a comprehensive list of necessary repairs and renovations. Obtain quotes from reliable contractor and estimate the costs of materials and labor. Update the budget for the rehab process, taking into account all necessary repairs and renovations, materials, labor. If you hadn't done so in the Estimate phase, be sure to add the 10 to 15 percent contingency for any unexpected expenses that may arise. Ensure that the cash-out and cash flow numbers still work.

There may be items that come up during home inspection that were not in your original budget (for example, there is termite damage in the basement that you contractor had not identified). In this case, get an estimate for removing termite, and any repair work needed as a result. Because you have a due-diligence contingency in your offer, you can go back to the seller and re-negotiate the purchase price to cover for this expense.

PHASE 3: FINALIZE

The Finalize phase of your rehab budget begins after you close on the property but before paying your contractor a deposit to start the work. To finalize the quote, review the detailed estimate provided by the contractor and ensure that all necessary repairs and renovations are included. If there are any discrepancies or additional expenses, discuss them with the contractor to come to a mutual agreement.

When a contractor provides an initial estimate, they may not be aware of all the necessary repairs and renovations until they start the work.

You want the contractor to assess the condition of the electrical and plumbing systems, as well as any structural components such as studs, beams, or joists. The process may involve cutting a small hole in the drywall or removing some sections of the wall to expose the underlying structure. This step is crucial for identifying any potential issues or necessary repairs that may not be immediately apparent from a visual inspection. By uncovering hidden problems, the contractor can make a more accurate estimate of the cost and time required to complete the rehab project and ensure that all necessary repairs are made.

If there are some surprises that come up during this process, you have the ability to adjust your repairs. For example, during the Finalize phase, you find that one of the rooms will need all new electrical work, that was not originally a part of the budget. Instead of finding this out near the end of the project and having to allocate your contingency budget toward this expense, you now have the ability to re-work your budget. You may choose to eliminate a "nice-to-have" item in your budget, such as putting in new flooring instead of salvaging the original hardwood floors. This way, you will still have the contingency in case of other surprises along the way.

This framework has saved us tens of thousands of dollars in multiple projects.

TYPICAL REHAB COSTS

Now let's talk about the typical rehab costs involved, and how much you can expect to pay for rehabbing a single-family three-bedroom, one-bathroom home that is around 1,000 sq. ft. Note that this may vary depending on labor costs in your area and quality of materials. Certain miscellaneous items such as basement parging, lighting, doors, structural work, and pest control are not included here and may need to be added as needed.

Kitchen	Cabinets, appliances, countertops, plumbing, flooring, backsplash	$12,000–$15,000
Bathroom	Vanity, toilet, tub/shower, plumbing, flooring	$8,000–$10,000
Roof	New roof	$2,500–$5,000
Flooring	Salvaging original hardwood flooring by sanding, staining and two coats of polyurethane OR Installing new luxury vinyl plank flooring	$2,500–$6,000
Paint	Interior and exterior	$2,500–$5,000
Windows	As needed, including material (window) and labor (installation)	$250–600 per window
Electrical	All new electrical if needed or a new electrical panel	$2,500–$6,000
Water Heater		$800–$1,000
Boiler / HVAC		$2,500–$6,000

PROJECT SCOPE

Project scope is all about identifying the extent of rehab you will need to perform in order for the house to get the ARV that you are looking for.

THE GOLDILOCKS PRINCIPLE

One of the mistakes we see new investors making is that they either (a) take on a project that barely needs any rehab, or (b) they go the other extreme and take on a project that is way too extensive for their first rehab project.

That is why we created the Goldilocks principle. The idea of the Goldilocks principle is that you take on a rehab project that is not too heavy, and not too light. Here's an example.

Goldilocks Zone for Project Scope

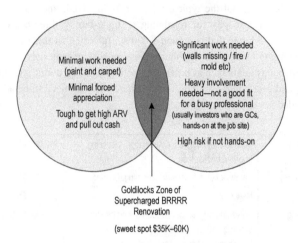

Too light: An example of this is a property that is move-in ready, and only needs paint and flooring. In this scenario, it would be hard to justify a high After Repair Value without showing a dramatic improvement in the property.

Too heavy: An example of this is a property with missing exterior walls, extensive fire damage, or heavy mold. A project such as this may be profitable, but it would be risky for a new investor to under-take.

So, what's the answer? You guessed it—not too heavy, not too light, just right! We will cover costs associated with different rehab items later in this chapter. Keep the Goldilocks principle in mind during the Estimate phase of budgeting to make sure you are picking the right property.

REHABBING FOR THE TWO KEY STAKEHOLDERS

There are two key stakeholders that you should keep in mind as you rehab your property. The first is tenant, and the second is the appraiser. You want to make sure your rehabbed property would be in line with the other rentals in the neighborhood, and that the rehab would justify the ARV, so that you can pull most, if not all, of your cash out.

Let's talk about both:

1. REHABBING TO SATISFY THE NEEDS OF YOUR TENANT

In order to satisfy your potential tenant, you want to make sure your property has the amenities that tenants commonly look for in the neighborhood. For example, if most rental properties in your neighborhood include a washer and dryer, you might want to include those amenities in order to be competitive.

Another example is that if other rentals in your area offer central air, you may want to provide that as well. On the flip side, if most rentals in your area don't have a finished basement, you could save money by not finishing your basement.

You can easily do this research in Zillow Rentals or other rental websites, looking specifically at the amenities that other rentals offer in the area.

2. REHABBING TO SATISFY YOUR APPRAISER TO GET A GOOD ARV

Being able to pull all or most of your money from your project is reliant upon getting a high ARV for your property.

When you start the Refinance part to pull your money out, the bank will send an appraiser to assess the after-repair value of the property. (Note: We cover appraisals in more detail later in the book.)

In order to justify a high appraisal, you want to do sufficient rehab. Here is what we typically rehab to get a good appraisal:

- **Kitchen:** New cabinets, new countertops, new flooring, and new appliances
- **Bathroom:** New flooring, new plumbing, new shower, vanity, and toilet
- **Roof:** Roof repair if it is in good condition, or replace it if it is in poor condition
- **Flooring:** Salvage original hardwood flooring, or if new flooring is needed, use good quality laminate or vinyl
- **Electric, Plumbing, and Mechanicals:** Bring electrical work up to code (if needed), fix leaks or update plumbing when renovating kitchen/bathroom, replace any mechanicals that are on their last leg

We typically spend between $40,000 and $70,000 on rehabbing a single-family home, depending on the condition of the property. Your rehab budget may vary based on the labor and material costs in the area you're investing in.

CONTINGENCY FOR YOUR REHAB

Last, it's important to plan for surprises in your rehab. Surprises can arise even following a thorough inspection. We recommend setting aside 10 to 15 percent of your budget for potential issues. Having contingency money can save your rehab project in case of theft, potential natural hazards, or other unexpected issues.

While we were closing the deal for a property in North Philadelphia, our real estate agent advised us to change the locks. He told us that too many people had keys to the property. Unfortunately, we decided to postpone this task to the next day since the construction work was scheduled to begin in the morning. When my contractor arrived on site, however, he discovered that thieves had broken in during the night.

He was also surprised by how unrattled we were. We already had a contingency plan that accounted for the losses involved. And we focused on the silver lining of the situation—we had learned a lesson we wouldn't forget. Always change the locks after closing a deal.

Of course, the lessons didn't end there. And since we approached real estate investing like a college student, we documented everything we learned from the beginning. Our meticulous notes helped me to remember all of our mistakes and improve on our course of action.

Eventually, we reached a point where we didn't need highly detailed project plans. With the systems, processes, and teams in place, we bought six properties while visiting family overseas.

FINDING AND VETTING A GENERAL CONTRACTOR

A lot of investors want to DIY their rehab projects. You might save money this way, but you would also spend a lot of your time on the site, or at Home Depot. Additionally, if you're doing all the rehab yourself, it may take you significantly longer, limiting the number of projects you can do.

When we started investing, we were very clear that we did not want to spend majority of our time at the job site. In fact, we built our business in a way that we don't ever have to visit our jobsite. Yes, we wanted to build wealth, but we also wanted time and location freedom! We didn't want to go from one nine-to-five job to another by doing all the rehab ourselves.

We wanted to leverage other people's time. This way, we could scale a lot faster. A general contractor with a crew of eight workers can rehab a single-family home in four to six weeks. DIY would take us months—and we would have to acquire a skill we didn't have and didn't need.

So, we decided early on that we would hire a contractor for the rehab.

There are many ways to hire contractors for a rehab project. You could hire subcontractors who have their areas of expertise; for example, electrician, plumber, contractor, etc. Or you could hire an all-in-one general contractor.

Hiring a general contractor is typically more expensive than hiring subcontractors. This is because when you hire a general contractor, they are responsible for hiring, coordinating, and managing the subcontractors. And it's the general contractor's responsibility to ensure that the quality of the subcontractors' work is good.

We didn't want to be in a situation where we had to hire and manage different subcontractors, because again, we wanted time and location freedom. This is why we hired a general contractor, and if you want time and location freedom, so should you!

HOW TO CHOOSE THE RIGHT CONTRACTOR FOR THE WORK

Before we started doing the BRRRR strategy, our first rental property was a rent-ready rental. The property was close to where we lived and had been renovated top-to-bottom by a house flipper.

At the closing table, we met the seller, who had flipped a couple of other properties as well. After closing, we were in the elevator with the seller, telling him how we really liked the quality of the rehab. We went a step further and asked if he would mind sharing the contact information for his contractor. To our utter delight, he said he certainly would.

We have worked with that contractor ever since, and he has rehabbed almost every property we have owned. He has helped us build a multi-million-dollar rental portfolio.

The reason we shared the story is because when you are looking for a contractor, it is so powerful to ask other investors for recommendations. And you don't have to just ask investors, you can ask property management companies, real estate agents, home inspectors, or lenders. Real Estate networking events (in-person or online) are great avenues to find contractors as well.

The key is to reach out to multiple contractors and get quotes from at least two or three so you can compare before choosing who to work with.

TWO PRO TIPS

No. 1 Don't Choose the Cheapest General Contractor!
While it's good to find an affordable contractor, it's important not to choose a contractor just because they promise they can do the work for half the price! If they are charging significantly less, they may compromise on the quality of the job or bid low upfront, only to add more charges later. It's important to find a contractor who is reasonably priced and provides realistic estimates for the rehab.

Always ask for at least two references from previous clients the contractor has worked with before. Talking to their references is a great way to find out if they finish their projects on time, on budget, and that their work is of good quality.

No. 2 Look Online to Find a General Contractor
It is true that general contractors don't spend a lot of time online. In fact, you'd probably rather work with a contractor who is always on the jobsite making sure the rehab goes well.

But with the power of internet, you can still find general contractors online, and one of the best ways is joining local investor Facebook groups, with some groups having 5,000 or more real estate investors. Asking for general contractor references on these groups is a great way to find your ideal contractor.

You might also consider visiting Zillow and look at recently renovated homes that are either for sale or have sold recently. Some county websites will let you look up the address and find permits that were pulled for the rehab, which should list the name of the contractor. This is another great way to find contractors who are doing work in the neighborhood.

HOW TO VET A CONTRACTOR

Once you have found a few contractors that work in your neighborhood, you want to get them to make sure they are a good fit and reliable.

To vet a contractor for a rehab project, follow these steps:

- **Licensed and Insured:** Verify that the contractor has the appropriate General Contractor license and is adequately insured. Before rehab work begins, you should ask them to add your LLC as an additional insured in their insurance policy.
- **References:** As you would before hiring any vendor, make sure to ask for references from previous clients and call those references to ensure that the contractor has a history of completing projects on time and on budget.
- **Prior Projects:** Review the contractor's portfolio of completed projects. Look to see if they have done similar projects to the one you are hiring them for.
- **Communication:** Communication and responsiveness are paramount. A good contractor should be willing to answer your questions and address any concerns you may have. If they seem flaky in your initial communications with them, that is a red flag.

- **Quotes:** Get detailed rehab quotes from at least three contractors and compare them to ensure that the prices are fair and reasonable. You can also use the other quotes as leverage to negotiate with the contractor you decide to work with.
- **Site Visit:** We covered this in the three phases of rehab estimation. Have the contractor visit the site to assess the project and identify any potential issues that may impact the cost or timeline.

By following these steps, you can effectively vet a contractor for a rehab project and ensure that they have the necessary experience and communication skills to complete the work efficiently and effectively. And remember, always trust your gut when vetting any vendors!

MANAGING THE REHAB PROJECT AT SCALE

As we mentioned earlier, when we started investing, we had a clear end-goal. Other than building generational wealth, we also wanted time and location freedom. We didn't want to be at the jobsite every day to manage the rehab. That is why we went the general contractor route. But we also didn't want the quality of our rehabs to suffer.

So, we built systems and processes to manage our rehab process that allowed us to be remote. We could be anywhere in the world and still have a good handle on the rehab process.

LEVERAGING PROCESSES USING THE 3T FRAMEWORK

TEMPLATES

Templates are a simple but powerful way to scale this business with ease. Create a template of finishes that you can use for every one of your rehab projects. Our general contractor knows exactly what flooring, kitchen cabinets, granite countertop, and appliances we like to use. He knows what paint color we like to use. Even the bathroom tiles and vanity are always the same. All of these items were the ones we identified over a period of time; these were inexpensive but still durable. You can go to www.biggerpockets.com/acceleratebonus to download the list of finishes we use for our renovations.

Having the exact same finishes in every house makes it very easy for our general contractor to order materials and install them. There is absolutely no guesswork!

We once purchased three duplexes and a single-family house while we were visiting our family in India. And because we had these templates and materials in place, our general contractor was able to do the rehab without us having to visit the property even once.

There are multiple advantages of this approach:

- **Profitability:** As you scale and take on multiple rehab projects at the same time, this approach helps in buying materials for cheaper in bulk.
- **Predictability:** Having a template of finishes makes budgeting and ARV predictable.
- **Time Savings:** This takes the guess work out and saves time at our end and the contractor's end. He knows what to order without having to run it by us again and again for every project.

TIMELINE

In order to finish multiple rehab projects successfully, you have to ensure that you are keeping a good handle on the timeline.

Create a Gantt chart in Excel to establish a timeline for the project with your contractor and track progress regularly. A Gantt chart is a graphical representation of a project schedule represented by horizontal bars on a timeline, where the length of each bar represents the duration of a task in the project. Start by creating a breakdown of the project scope.

	In Progress											
	Delayed											
	Completed											
	X			6/21	6/28	7/5	7/12	7/19	7/26| 8/2	8/9	8/16	8/23
		Start Date	End Date									
Permits	Obtaining Permits											
Demo	Demo											
	Demo and removal of debris and belongings	6/28										
Exterior	Exterior											
	Roof											
	Other exterior											
	Doors And Windows											
Interior	Interior											
	Flooring											
	Paint											
	Drywall/Sheetrock/framing											
	Electrical											
	Plumbing Rough/Final/Fixtures											
	Water heater											
Kitchen	Kitchen 1											
	Cabinets											
	Counters											
	Appliances											
Bath 1	Bath 1											
	Tile/flooring											
	Vanity											
	Bath/toilet											
Other	Other											

If you are intimated by the idea of creating a Gantt chart for a project scope, here are some tips. You can get on the phone with your contractor and tell him you are trying to keep up with the project schedule and are just trying to get a feel for what his method would be. What would he tackle first (usually the exterior and the roof) and so on and so forth. List the tasks at a high level in the order in which they need to be completed. Remember, we are trying to work on this at a high level to have an overall feel for the process.

Determine the start and end dates for each task. The end date for each task should be the start date of the following task. Some tasks will overlap if your contractor has a decent size crew. Insert a stacked bar chart in Excel or a similar tool. Add the data for each task to the chart. Use the start and end dates to determine the duration of each task. For each task, create a stacked bar that represents the duration of the task. Add milestones to the chart to mark key events in the project, such as permits. Update the chart regularly to reflect changes in the project plan or timeline. This will help you stay on top of the project's progress and ensure that it is completed on time.

We often joke that the first rule in project management is to take the timeline a contractor gives you and add 20 percent additional time to it to get a more realistic idea on completion. This is partially a joke, but it is also a reality. In our experience with new investors, it could potentially even be more than 20 percent. Managing your expectations will allow you to maintain a good relationship with your contractor.

TRACKING BUDGET

One of the biggest challenges new investors face is not being able to track their rehab budget accurately on an ongoing basis. This is because there are many transactions for all the materials being purchased, and when doing multiple projects simultaneously, it can get tricky for them to be consistently allocated to the right projects. This can be solved by using a tool such as Trello or Asana specifically for tracking the budget. You can create board which can include a list of expenses, such as materials, labor, permits, and miscellaneous costs. The next step is to assign a budget for each expense and add it as a sub-task under the appropriate task in the project board. This will allow you to track the actual cost of the task against the budgeted cost. One thing we cannot stress enough is to regularly monitor spending to ensure that you are staying within the budget.

Your contractor may be a small business with not a lot of back-end office support. He is not usually doing desk work as he spends his days at the jobsite. Take the lead on keeping track of the budget so you can make sure your project is moving forward smoothly. You can use labels or color codes in Asana or Trello to indicate whether a task is on budget, over budget, or under budget.

Create checklists to track expenses, payments, and invoices. This will help you stay organized and ensure that all expenses are accounted for. Last, update the budget board regularly to reflect changes in expenses or changes in the project scope. This will help you stay on top of the budget and avoid any surprises. Regularly review the budget with the contractor—this helps to make sure he has an ongoing feel for how the budget is moving forward in comparison to the progress.

LEVERAGING SYSTEMS

VIDEO WALKTHROUGHS

Communication is key when managing a rehab project remotely. Use video conferencing tools that can easily be accessed over the phone such as WhatsApp or FaceTime to regularly discuss the project with your contractor. This will allow you to see the work that's being done and make sure that it's being done to your satisfaction. In addition, if you are investing remotely, you can leverage your boots on the ground person to visit the rehab project once a week. We will talk more about this in the next section.

Earlier, we mentioned how we acquired properties while we were overseas. To manage the project, we did video walk-throughs with our general contractor at least once a week. This is a great way for our GC to show us the progress on the rehab, and we can ask him questions as needed. The video walk-throughs worked so well to ensure progress that we made them a part of every rehab project we do.

GOOGLE DRIVE/DROPBOX

Keeping organized records and documents for easy reference and future use will allow you to keep your sanity, avoid any confusion, and be on the same page as your contractor at all times. This will be even more impactful when managing multiple rehabs at the same time. Be sure to create folders and naming conventions that are easily searchable. The key to an organized business is document control. In addition to what we discussed in the processes section of this chapter, here are some of the essential documents you needed to effectively manage a renovation project:

- **Proof of License and Insurance:** Make sure that the contractor provides proof of his license and insurance before starting work

on the project. This should include liability insurance and workers' compensation insurance.
- **Contractor Agreement:** This outlines the terms of the contract between you and the contractor. This may include the scope of work, payment schedule, and timeline. It should also include information about change management and termination of the contract.
- **Invoice:** The contractor should provide an invoice for each payment that is due. The invoice should include the amount due, a description of the work completed, and the date the payment is due. The invoices are critical in making sure you are both on the same page as the project moves forward.
- **Lien waiver:** At the end of the project, the contractor a lien waiver may be requested from the contractor. The lien waiver certifies that the contractor has been paid for the work completed and that they will not file a lien against the property.

Make sure that you review each document carefully before signing and keep a copy of all documents for your records.

LEVERAGING TEAMS

Having a "boots on the ground" person who can act as your eyes and ears is extremely useful when it comes to overseeing the rehab. This person can visit the jobsite on a regular basis and take videos/pictures to send to you. They can also provide you with updates on whether the rehab is being done on schedule.

REAL ESTATE AGENT

Someone with basic construction knowledge that can simply use their phone to provide videos and photos to you on a regular basis can prove to be a valuable asset to scaling your business. We have had great luck working with up-and-coming agents who are looking to make some additional income on the side.

HARD MONEY LOAN INSPECTOR

Hard money lenders are a great resource for financing the rehab for your projects. But one of the added benefits of working with a hard money lender (HML) is that they can also be your eyes and ears for the rehab project. When a portion of the rehab is finished, your HML will send an inspector to the property to ensure that the rehab has indeed been completed. Once the inspector gives their stamp of approval, the HML will send you the funds so that you can pay your contractor. Having the inspector (who is independent of the general contractor) visit the property is a great way to ensure that the rehab is progressing well. We'll go into more details on Hard Money Lending later in this book.

HANDYPERSON

A great place to find a handyperson is www.taskrabbit.com. You can also find local boots on the ground via websites like www.wegolook.com.

By building a team that you can leverage, you can effectively manage a rehab project with your contractor remotely. It's important to maintain open communication and stay on top of the project's progress to ensure that the work is completed on time and within budget.

Explain exactly what you would scrutinize during every walkthrough. From there, your team would handle taking pictures of the electrical panels, the plumbing and heating systems, ask specific questions, and so on. You can get all the details you'd need without being present to look at properties.

NEVER PAY THE ENTIRE REHAB AMOUNT TO THE CONTRACTOR UPFRONT!

One of the big mistakes we see new investors make is to pay a large amount to the contractor upfront. This almost always ends badly for the investor.

I recommend working out a structure which pays as the work progresses. You may also consider providing a small upfront payment to cover materials for the first portion of the project, and then only pay the contractor as each phase of the rehab is completed. We typically make three to four payments to the contractor over the course of the rehab process.

With careful consideration, cooperation, and continuous communication, finding and building a long-term relationship with the right contractor is possible. Most importantly, it can be a key piece to building your own real estate investment business.

MEET ROCKSTAR INVESTOR NANCY

Before, Nancy was content with doing turnkey deals. She would typically only do one or two deals per year, and she was content with this situation. However, once Nancy shifted her approach to a more scalable model, she gained confidence and is now comfortable doing ten to twenty doors per year. Not only that, but she also diversified her portfolio.

Initially, buying turnkey properties seemed like enough. However, once Nancy figured out how to rehab a property from a distance, she doesn't mind doing it repeatedly, and she has made it her new lifestyle. This is a significant improvement from her initial position when she had several doors but couldn't further scale her investments.

On one of the first deals, Nancy bought a $65,000 property and estimated the rehab costs at around $40,000. However, her contractor actually came in at $37,000, which was great as the estimated ARV was around $150,000.

Nancy is now enjoying her game of real-life Monopoly in her area. Her most exciting moment wasn't seeing how her life changed so far. Instead, it was seeing the potential for exponential change and growth as she continues to use the same process.

CHAPTER SEVEN
Adding Cash Flow (Rent)

Cash flow is king! Cash flow from your properties is what will help you replace your nine-to-five income. And one of the reasons we love buying and holding onto properties for a long period of time is because cash flow increases over time.

Since cash flow is critical to your success as in investor, it is important to understand not only the basics of how to rent the property but also how you can maximize your cash flow as your scale your portfolio—without having to answer any late-night tenant phone calls.

This is where systems, processes, and teams become the most crucial. In this chapter, we will discuss the steps involved in managing your properties and how to maximize your cash flow. This process can be divided into five key steps: marketing, showings, screening, leasing, and property management.

MARKETING

In order to get the best rents, as well as great tenants, you will need to market your property well.

- Set a competitive rent price that maximizes cash flow: A lot of new investors may not have a good idea of what their property could rent for. In this case, you should research the local rental market to determine a competitive rent price that will generate maximum rental income for your property. We typically use Zillow to identify rents in the neighborhood. Consider any unique features or amenities of your property that could allow you to charge a premium price.
- Prepare the property for marketing to attract quality tenants: Before showing the property to potential tenants, ensure that it is clean and

professionally photographed. This can help attract high-quality tenants who are willing to pay a premium rent.
- Create a stand-out listing: Websites like Zillow, Trulia, and Apartments.com can help you advertise your rental to a broad audience, offering features like virtual tours, photos, and floor plans to help potential tenants get a sense of the property. Make sure your rental listing is accurate, detailed, and includes high-quality photos. Many property management software will syndicate the listing across various websites and can save you time and money.

SHOWINGS

In the previous step, we discussed how to maximize high-quality leads for your property. In this step, we will discuss how to track all the leads and quickly move them to the next step. Handling the leads quickly and efficiently has a direct impact on cash flow because it allows you to quickly get your property rented, reduce vacancies, and get the best quality tenants.

- Schedule and conduct showings efficiently to minimize vacancy: Respond to inquiries and schedule showings for potential tenants promptly to minimize the time the property is vacant. We usually start marketing our properties sixty days before the end of the lease of the existing tenant. This allows for ample time to find a new tenant, ultimately reducing vacancies.
- Consider open houses as opposed to individual showings, allowing you to maximize your time.
- Conduct showings in a professional manner and provide potential tenants with all necessary information about the property to ensure they can make an informed decision. This can be outsourced to a team member as you scale.
- When we discuss systems and processes, we will go over our no contact showing process. This has allowed the time it took to lease a property from weeks to days. Born during COVID-19 as a necessity, this process has been an amazing addition to our repertoire.

SCREENING

In our experience, many new investors are wary of committing to real estate for one reason: tenants. You'll always hear horror stories involving tenants, perhaps more so than encouraging tales. In reality, you can avoid these horror stories by implementing a reliable screening process.

Our ideal tenants are those that pay rent on time and maintain the property. Implementing best practices in tenant screening is critical for ensuring that you find reliable and trustworthy renters for your property. To achieve this, it is essential to develop a thorough tenant screening process that is consistent, clear, and comprehensive in covering all aspects of the tenant's background.

IMPORTANCE OF SCREENING

There are two things that can impact your cash flow significantly: high vacancy rates and a tenant that destroys your property. They might seem unrelated, but they are two sides of the same coin. Let me explain.

The words "vacancy rate" causes real estate investors to break out in a cold sweat, and rightly so. A high vacancy rate can blow a hole in your profits and cash flow. Needless to say, filling up vacancies as soon as possible is the top priority for landlords, to the extent that the fear of any delay causes most landlords to drop their guard.

They tend to ignore due diligence while screening tenants. As a result, they end up with problem renters, a scenario that might possibly lead to evictions and legal disputes. These issues can result in a greater damage to their cash flow, as well as causing mental agony. It is for this reason that we strongly recommend a thorough tenant screening. The good news is that there are tools which make tenant screening extremely easy, fast, and hassle-free.

In this guide, we will discuss the most important factors to consider when screening rental applications and also provide some actionable tips on how to do it the right way.

CRITERIA

Looking at a tenant's rental history can help you differentiate between an ideal tenant and a problematic one. There are five criteria that we take into consideration when doing a background check. (Note: When screening tenants, it is essential to ensure that your process is compliant with all applicable local laws, particularly those related to fair housing. If you are unsure of any of the ideas discussed below, do consider consulting with a local attorney or fair housing agency to ensure that you are following all laws and regulations in your area.)

1. Payment Discipline
To ensure that the potential tenant will likely pay rent on time, you need to verify employment history and credit report. The tenant should be able

to afford the rent, and the only way to determine this is to find out his or her current financial situation. You need to ensure that the rental application carries all the necessary information and documents including the approval for you to pull their credit report and the name, address, and phone number of the current and former employers. One of our requirements is that a potential tenant's income should be three times the rent.

2. Treatment of Your Property

Your ideal tenants should treat your property like their own. The question remains how to find out whether a tenant satisfies this requirement, and the simple solution is to contact his or her previous landlords and get their feedback. We make sure that our tenants furnish details of their current and previous landlords including their name, address, and contact numbers.

3. Length of Stay

While screening tenants, you need to predict the length of their stay. Rental turnover can have a significant impact on your rental income in the long run. A high tenant retention rate will ensure a low vacancy rate and also reduce overhead costs caused whenever a rental unit falls vacant, including time consuming and costly tenant screening process. The best way to predict the length of your rental applicant's stay is to check how long they stayed in each of their previous rentals. A tenant who has a history of vacating rentals frequently by breaking their lease is less likely to remain at your property for a long time. In order to find out how long your prospective tenants stayed in each of their previous rental homes, you will need to have details of their landlords or property management agencies and contact them.

4. Nuisance to Neighbors

A rental home is a temporary accommodation, so some tenants aren't keen on developing social ties and tend to take their neighbors for granted. Make sure that your potential tenants are going to be a good neighbor, particularly if you are managing a multifamily residential property. Previous landlord references can help you verify this.

5. Eviction and Criminal History

Last but not the least, check the potential tenant's eviction history and criminal background, provided you are allowed to screen for that in your area. Most tenants who were evicted by their previous landlords hide this fact in their rental applications. It's a landlord's responsibility to dig into the national criminal and eviction databases.

TIPS

- Certain criteria for tenant screening varies by neighborhood. For example, expecting a credit score of 740 in some neighborhoods or for certain property types may not be feasible.
- Many tenants who can't provide landlord references and employment history offer to arrange for rental lease co-signers with a good credit history. However, it's up to you whether want to accept cosigners in place of income proof and landlord references. For example, if the majority of your rental applicants are adult students, you can't expect them to have a stellar credit score or a long employment history.
- Make sure that the prospective tenant has attached two or three most recent pay stubs. This will help not only you verify employment but also ensure that your tenant will be able to afford the rent. The income should be at least three times the rent.
- Collect copies of identification documents such as a driver's license.

USEFUL TEMPLATES

While the tools mentioned in this guide will help you conduct a credit, criminal background, and eviction history check, you will still need to manually verify employment and rental history.

1. Verifying Employment

To save time when verifying employment every time you screen rental applications, you can create an email template or a form to send out to the employers. However, we recommend that you speak to the employers over phone to make sure that the person referenced in the rental application is real. This would be difficult to determine through email verification.

Make sure that you send a written consent of the applicant to the employer authorizing you to seek financial and personal information. This is particularly applicable if you are seeking information over phone.

A credit report corroborates a person's employment history, so in case the employer refuses to disclose the information you are seeking, you can get the details of the applicant's salary, existing financial liabilities, and income from the credit report.

Keep in mind that any bogus reference in the rental application should be treated as a warning sign. You should think twice about renting to a person who has knowingly lied in the rental application. The onus of verifying the authenticity of the references is entirely on you.

2. Verifying Rental Background

You can create a templated form to send to the rental applicant's current and previous landlords for rental history verification.

In some cases, the landlords you contact for rental background verification may not be able to reply by fax or email. In that case, you can mail them an envelope with the return address (along with the verification form). You can request them to send the form back by mail using that envelope.

PHILOSOPHY OF HOSPITALITY

Our philosophy around property management, which we have implemented and train our team on, is that of hospitality.

Over the past few years, we've come to realize that managing one's own properties isn't just to save money, it has other advantages as well. With process streamlining and outsourcing key elements of property management, the tenant/landlord relationship can be something an investor can maintain without a lot of time commitment.

In entrepreneurship, having a heartfelt "connection" isn't given the importance it deserves in a business relationship. After all, it should be all about the numbers, right?

What if we told you that you can feel fulfilled at the end of the day while making money? Establishing and maintaining a tenant/landlord relationship can be a very rewarding experience, considering the property owner is providing housing for someone and helping them build their life. Granted, there are exceptions, but overall, most tenants want to feel safe, comfortable, and be heard.

The screening process is actually simple, but it's the preparation or first step that takes the most time.

1. Create your criteria
2. Perform a brief initial screening
3. Build an application
4. Screen prospects based on the application
5. Make your decision

If you happen to hire property managers with more experience than you, which many rookie investors do, then use their knowledge to come up with the best screening policies for your properties.

LEASING

Screen potential tenants per our earlier advice to ensure that they meet your rental requirements, including their ability to pay rent on time and their willingness to take care of the property. A high-quality tenant will help minimize turnover and lost rental income. Next, an efficient leasing process that generates high cash flow is critical for maximizing your rental property's profitability. To achieve this, you must focus on the following key steps:

Draft a lease agreement that maximizes rental income. Draft a lease agreement that clearly outlines the terms and conditions of the rental agreement. Ensure that the rental amount is set at a premium price that maximizes your rental income while still being reasonable for the tenant. Be sure to take your local laws into account when drafting a lease. It is advisable to hire an attorney to review your lease.

Collect security deposit and first month's rent promptly to ensure cash flow. Collect the security deposit (usually equal to one month's rent) and first month's rent promptly before the tenant moves in to ensure a steady cash flow. In many states, you are allowed to also ask for the last month's rent on top of the security deposit and first month's rent. Possession is provided to the tenant when these are received.

PROPERTY MANAGEMENT

Efficient property management for rental properties can be broken down into three key steps: tenant onboarding, ongoing maintenance, and end of lease management.

TENANT ONBOARDING

Tenant onboarding is the first step in efficient property management, where new tenants are welcomed to the property and given a clear understanding of the property's rules, regulations, and procedures. This includes providing a thorough walkthrough of the property, outlining maintenance expectations and contact information for emergency repairs, and providing tenants with copies of the lease agreement and other important documents.

Many new investors don't have tenant onboarding in place. The experience of your tenant in the property throughout the term of their lease can be enhanced by a good onboarding experience. Clear expectations setting with the tenant gives them clarity on (a) how they can reach out in case of non-emergency repairs, (b) emergency contact information (more on this later in this chapter), and (c) typical response time for repairs. Having a clearly laid out onboarding process is key to maintaining a good tenant-landlord relationship.

ONGOING MAINTENANCE

Ongoing maintenance is critical for ensuring that the property remains in good condition throughout the lease term, and that your tenant is happy. This may include regular inspections (we recommend every six months), preventive maintenance (for example, servicing of roof, HVAC, etc.), and prompt resolution of repair requests. Landlords must have a clear process for handling repair requests, including emergency repairs, and should ensure that all maintenance work is performed by qualified and licensed professionals.

END OF LEASE MANAGEMENT

As the lease term comes to an end, the investor must take steps to ensure a smooth transition. This includes having a team member conduct a final walkthrough to assess the property's condition and providing tenants with clear move-out instructions. Once the tenant has moved out, assess any damages or necessary repairs and return the security deposit, subtracting any deductions for damages or unpaid rent.

With a thorough onboarding process, ongoing maintenance, and clear end-of-lease procedures, property managers can provide a high-quality rental experience for tenants while maintaining the property's value and profitability.

LEVERAGING FRAMEWORKS, SYSTEMS, AND TOOLS

TENANT ACQUISITION FUNNEL

Looking at tenant acquisition as a funnel can help investors understand and optimize the process of acquiring new tenants. A funnel is a visual representation of the customer journey, from the initial awareness of a product or service to the final conversion into a customer. By breaking down the tenant acquisition process into specific steps, you can identify potential bottlenecks and areas for improvement. This allows you to streamline the process and improve its efficiency, ultimately leading to increased cash flow.

The reason we like to think of this as a funnel is that it helps pinpoint problems more accurately if the property is hard to rent. A high vacancy rate can be a major blow to the Net Operation Income (NOI). A poor NOI will have a negative impact on almost every aspect of your investment goals. It not only reduces cash flow but also decrease the property's market value.

Tenant Acquisition Funnel

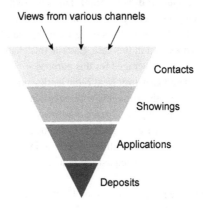

The funnel above is a visual representation of the various stages involved in the tenant acquisition funnel. Below are the steps in the funnel:

1. Views of Property Listing: The first stage in the tenant acquisition funnel is preparing a great rental listing for the property in order to maximize views. Most tenants start their search for a rental online. Since the property listing websites are inundated with rental listings, you need to grab potential tenants' attention with a great listing. This involves getting great professional photos of the property after renovation and including a high-quality and detailed description of the property listing the location, amenities, and key features to increase the views on your listings.

2. Contact: Once you set up a desirable listing, you will likely receive a lot of interest in the property. You will need to manage the leads that are reaching to you to view the property, which can be done by responding promptly to inquiries and providing a clear process for viewing the property, submitting an application, and signing a lease agreement.

3. Showings: The next step is to schedule showings for interested leads. This can be done either through individual appointments, open houses, or no-contact showings (discussed later in this chapter). The goal for this step is to ensure that you make it easier for your tenants to schedule a showing and view the property. Are there a lot of steps before showing? Are you showing often enough? Is your audience older and you're expecting them to use tech? Is your audience a church going group and you're only showing on Sunday? You will need iterations to figure this out! This will make showings more convenient and hassle-free for prospective renters.

4. Applications and Screening: The next step is getting applications and having a screening process in place. Having a clear list of items needed from the tenant and a simple form that can be used to upload these items works well in this case. Later in this chapter, we will discuss software that can be leveraged for this purpose.

5. Deposits and Leasing: Next is the leasing process. Be sure to make this process as smooth as possible with steps that are predictable and easy to follow. One of our biggest tips for new investors is to not stop showing a property until the lease is signed and a deposit has been received.

Here are a few tips you will find useful in implementing and making the most out of the tenant acquisition funnel:

- Appropriate rent: Drop the rent. Do this often by $10 increments to get your listing to show up as fresh again and closely monitor the conversions. When things suddenly pick up, that's when you know you've landed on your appropriate rent. This will also improve views on your listings.
- Responsiveness: Responding to feedback and questions and processing rental applications quickly is extremely important. Keep in mind that people usually view multiple properties. Your responsiveness can make you stand out from your competitors. Remember, you can sell an less-than-perfect product by combining it with top-notch service.
- Feedback: Feedback from potential tenants is GOLD. Get on the phone with the people who saw it but didn't apply—that way, you'll know why you aren't getting enough applications. This will help you come up with ways to improve conversion rate and get more applications.
- Managing Expectations: The tenant pool you're getting is what it is. You'll need to choose from that. You will need to align and figure out your screening criteria based on this pool or prospective renters.

LEVERAGING SYSTEMS

Here are a couple of tools that we recommend you use for the purpose of tenant screening:

SMARTMOVE BY TRANSUNION

TransUnion is one of the three credit rating agencies in the United States. Their web application—SmartMove—has been designed specifically for landlords, real estate investors, and property management agencies. SmartMove lets you access a tenant's credit score, eviction history, criminal background (if any), and income insight. Based on these factors, SmartMove rates tenants on its Credit-Based Resident Score scale.

PROPERTY MANAGEMENT SOFTWARE

I highly recommend that you use a property management software. There are multiple property management software programs that are free. When we first started, we used Cozy, which allows you to compare rental applications based on different criteria. After about twenty properties, we moved over to a paid option to be able to use all of the bells and whistles that a larger portfolio can benefit from and afford. One of the best ones out there is www.buildium.com. Buildium gives you access to a tenant's rental background, credit score, and eviction history, among other useful information.

There are many other paid and free tools available in the online marketplace which can make tenant screening extremely easy. Application of technology in tenant screening will not only save time and money, but it will also reduce chances of errors in human judgment.

BOOKKEEPING AND BILL PAYMENT SOFTWARE

Bookkeeping and bill payment software can be a powerful tool for investors, making property management more efficient. By using bookkeeping software to track income and expenses and manage financial reports, investors can streamline their accounting operations. By leveraging bill payment software, bills can be paid electronically and vendor relationships can be more easily managed. This saves time and reduces the risk of errors while also providing greater visibility into the income and expense for all your properties.

We prefer using Quickbooks for bookkeeping and Bill.com for automating bill payments. As you scale, your needs will change, and so will your choice of software.

LEVERAGING PROCESSES

LOCKBOX AT PROPERTY WITH KEYS

Having a lockbox at your rental property can be a convenient way to manage your property, especially if you live out of state. This makes it easy for your maintenance technician or handyman to access the property when repairs are needed and your tenant is not at home. Be sure to follow local laws and regulations regarding giving tenants proper notice prior to entry.

Consider installing the lockbox on a secure surface such as a fence post, railing, or other sturdy location near the front or back door. Maintain a Google Sheet with codes for all your properties or enter them in the notes section of your property management software.

Alternatively, you can invest in smart lockboxes that use wireless technology to allow remote access to the property. These lockboxes can be controlled with a smartphone app or other web-enabled device and offer features such as automatic code changing, time-limited access, and activity logs.

SELF-SHOWINGS: TENANT TURNER/SHOWMOJO

Let's discuss self-showings and how they work. When we first heard of virtual showings, we were skeptical, but the COVID-19 pandemic made it a necessity, and necessity is the mother of invention. Now, we use virtual showings almost exclusively and have found them to be highly effective.

If you're not familiar with self-showings, they are a way for potential tenants to physically visit a rental property without the presence of a landlord or property manager. Potential tenants are able to schedule a self-showing of the property and access the property, often using a lockbox with a code. There are companies who specialize in self-showings and have cloud-based tools and software. The process can be set up online, with potential tenants scheduling appointments to view the property. Some software even offers an automated phone option.

At first, the idea of self-showings may seem daunting, but they allow properties to be rented out while minimizing face-to-face contact. We suggest providing detailed instructions on how to safely enter properties, installing lockboxes with changing codes every fifteen minutes (such as Tenant Turner or ShowMojo), conducting soft background checks on potential tenants, and scheduling appointments with sufficient time intervals to avoid overlaps.

AFTER HOURS ANSWERING SERVICE

Managing tenant phone calls can be a time-consuming and disruptive task, particularly if you receive calls at odd hours. An effective solution for this is to use an answering service to handle late-night tenant phone calls. An answering service is a company that provides phone answering services on behalf of businesses and individuals. These services are typically available 24/7 and can handle a range of tasks, including taking messages, forwarding calls, and providing information to callers. Here is how you can leverage an answering service for late-night tenant phone calls:

- Research options for hiring an answering service: There are many answering services available, so it's important to choose one that meets your needs and budget. You can look for an answering service that has experience working with real estate investors and that can handle emergency calls 24/7.
- Provide instructions to the answering service: Once you've chosen an answering service, you'll need to provide them with instructions on how to handle tenant phone calls. This should include information on how to handle emergency calls, how to contact you or your property manager, and any other relevant information.
- Inform your tenants: Communicate to your tenants know that you have engaged an answering service to handle late-night phone calls. Provide them with the answering service's contact information and instructions on how to use the service.
- Monitor calls for quality: Periodically review the messages and information provided by the answering service to ensure that they are handling tenant phone calls effectively. Make adjustments as needed to improve the service and address any issues that arise.

LEVERAGING TEAMS

PROPERTY MANAGER

If you have limited time in a day, like we did when we got started, your best option is to hire a property management company to manage your property. But how do you choose a good property manager?

As cliché as it may sound, you need to value integrity above all else. You might be tempted to get someone with low fees in order to generate additional profit. However, every decision and action a property manager takes will directly affect your profit.

Therefore, if the property manager doesn't have your best interests at heart, they could do a poor job that will cost you your tenants and your money. Integrity will help you achieve a higher return on investment. Screen your property manager, have an in-person meeting, check their references, look for complaints. Do your due diligence. Once you can trust that person or company to collect rent, maintain relationships with tenants, and handle daily maintenance needs, you can be a hands-off landlord. That will help you focus more on growing your portfolio further.

Of course, once you become hands-off, you won't want to deal with advertising either. This means that your property manager should take care of that aspect. Analyze the property manager's current listings, how well they respond to ads, and how good they are at showcasing the best features of a property.

A full-service property manager should be a good salesperson. A good property management company should offer everything from rent collection to professional photography to help you get tenants faster and keep your vacancy rates low.

From there, you should also look at the documentation. Perhaps a property manager has terms you don't agree with, whether it's about leasing, termination clauses, fee percentages, etc.

But what about managing your own properties, if time allows it? Is it an option worth considering?

Yes.

All negotiations tend to go smoother when there are only two parties involved. The money you save, perhaps up to 10 percent of your rent, can be distributed between increasing your profits and making your tenants' lives easier by providing higher quality services.

Let's consider another aspect—fulfillment. If you choose to become an entrepreneur, financial goals aren't the only driving forces behind your decision, even as a real estate investor. Having a heartfelt connection with your business will make your journey more enjoyable. That's why some investors always try to be as hands-on as possible by maintaining the tenant-landlord relationship for as long as possible.

PHOTOGRAPHER

When it comes to marketing a rental property online to attract tenants, high-quality photographs are essential. One way to ensure that your rental property is properly captured is by hiring an experienced real estate photographer and creating a photography template for your rental property photographer. This template should include a list of photos to take, which will vary based on the unique features of the property.

The goal of the photography template is to ensure that the photographer captures the property in the best possible light, highlighting amenities and best features. Some photos to consider including in the template are exterior shots of the property, interior shots of each room, photos of unique features, such as a fireplace or a spacious closet, and photos of any outdoor amenities, such as a pool or a patio. By creating a photography template, you can ensure that the photographer captures all the necessary shots to showcase your rental property effectively and attract the right tenants.

CLEANING CREW

A professional cleaning is required before taking photographs of a rental property after it is renovated for several reasons. First, a professional cleaning can help to ensure that the property is presented in the best possible light. By removing dirt, debris, and other unsightly elements, a professional cleaning can make the property look a more attractive and appealing to potential tenants. This is particularly important for photographs, which will be the first point of contact for many potential tenants. By ensuring that the property is clean, safe, and attractive, landlords and property managers can increase their chances of attracting high-quality tenants and protecting their investment in the property.

On that note, let me introduce you to another real estate investor that overcame a rough start but followed this framework to become successful.

MEET ROCKSTAR INVESTOR JENNIFER

When Jennifer started her real estate investment journey, she had the same skepticism as most other newbies. But for her, it wasn't an issue of profitability and wealth generation potential. Coming from the health care industry with zero real estate investment experience, Jennifer believed that it might take her up to thirty-six months to learn acquisition, financing, rehab, and everything else that goes into the BRRRR strategy.

Initially, Jennifer didn't truly grasp the numbers involved in real estate investment deals and why they worked. Once she did, she gained the tools and confidence needed to quickly analyze deals and determine their profitability to fit her financial goals.

Jennifer had a tendency to overestimate her repairs on her first deals. She believed that making a property look rent-ready and great for future tenants could take up to $60,000. That all changed after Jennifer learned what to look for in a property based on what tenants want in her investment location.

That's when she understood that rehab or some repairs don't have to cost as much as the property itself to make it attractive to tenants. Everyone has specific expectations and needs. Cash flow–generating properties, or rentals, typically don't have the same beautification, modernization, or rehab requirements as homes you're buying to resale at a profit.

Jennifer had many "aha" moments like these during her first three months as an investor, making her more knowledgeable and confident when putting together profitable deals.

CHAPTER EIGHT
Leverage and Commercial Financing (Refinance)

Let's start with asking a fundamental question: What does refinancing an investment property mean?

The Refinance step involves obtaining a long-term mortgage loan on the property based on its after-repair value. If you had obtained short-term financing (or hard money financing) to purchase and rehab the property, the refinance will allow you to pay off the hard money loan. Remember, a hard money loan is typically for a short duration (e.g., six to twelve months). And refinancing the property will allow you to lock into a long-term mortgage.

Refinance is a critical part of the real estate investing strategy, as it allows investors to recover their initial investment and recycle the capital to buy more properties. The primary goal of the Refinance step is to recover as much of the initial investment as possible while still maintaining positive cash flow. The ideal scenario is to refinance the property at a higher value than the purchase price and renovation costs, resulting in a cash-out refinance. Typically, you would refinance the property after the rehab has been completed and after the property has been leased to a tenant.

FORTUNE FAVORS THE FINANCE SAVVY

As we discussed earlier, mastering deal analysis is critical to building a rental portfolio. However, without knowing how to finance your deals, it may take you a long time to scale.

There's a common misconception that you need money to make money. In our case, though, we didn't have a large amount of capital at our disposal when we first started out—we only had $25,000. Therefore, we had to learn how to leverage our money.

This was another huge mindset shift we had to make. As South Asians, we were raised to think that all debt is bad, and all debts must be paid off if you want to do well financially. In hindsight, this is not great advice if you want to become wealthy. Not all debt is bad debt. Yes, you should always pay off your credit card debt, car loan, and the like, but knowing how to leverage money for real estate can increase your returns four or even five times.

Borrowing money may sound scary, but you can avoid undesirable outcomes if you know what to expect. By treating your real estate venture like a business, you can scale your portfolio exponentially. If you want to truly scale your portfolio, you really need to understand two key things:

1) Using leverage to refinance and pull your cash out and to leverage capital to purchase and rehab the property.
2) Unlocking the growth potential of a portfolio using commercial finance.

UP-FRONT LEVERAGE

When we first started investing, we only knew of thirty-year fixed residential mortgages offered by traditional banks. However, traditional banks don't finance distressed houses. And so, when we decided to pursue growing a rental portfolio at scale, we thought we'd have to come up with our own cash to finance the purchase and renovation costs.

This would mean a substantial amount of cash of up to $150,000 for each deal, which would hinder scalability. Capital constraint is the number one reason why most people give up on building their rental portfolio. However, understanding and implementing up-front leverage will allow you to grow exponentially. This can be the single most tweak that can change an investor's trajectory from a mom-and-pop rental property investor to a business that can scale quickly with low risk.

Short-term financing allows you to finance both the purchase and the rehab costs for a property. It's a great way to finance a deal, without using a significant amount of your own cash.

There are many options for up-front leverage, such as private money, sub-to, owner financing, and hard money loans. In this section, we will take the guesswork out and show you why we eliminated majority of the up-front leverage strategies out there, narrowing our focus down to a single option that will help you scale fast with time freedom in mind. We will briefly mention the different funding options for up-front leverage but as with everything else in this book, we will show you the specific framework we have used to scale our business. This strategy has been replicated by hundreds of investors who have high-achieving professions and they have been able to execute it while having a full-time job and kids.

Here is a quick outline of different up-front leverage options available:

OWNER FINANCING/SUBJECT-TO

Owner Financing, also known as also known as seller financing, is a type of real estate transaction where the seller of a property acts as the lender and provides financing to the buyer. In owner financing, the investor obtains a loan directly from the seller, rather than obtaining a loan from a traditional lender such as a bank.

Subject-to financing involves the buyer taking over the seller's existing mortgage payments. In this arrangement, the buyer does not obtain a new loan, but rather takes over the seller's mortgage payments and assumes responsibility for the loan.

Here are some drawbacks to these two options for up-front leverage:

- High price for great terms: There is no such thing as a free lunch. When it comes to owner financing, as an investor, you may get good terms, such as bringing less capital to the table, but it comes at a price—pun intended. The advantage to the seller to offer great terms is a higher selling price.
- Capital for renovation: If we are trying to renovate the property to force appreciation, you will need to find a way to fund the renovation.
- Lack of systems and processes: Unless you are trying to build an entire business of owner-financed or subject-to properties, this will require you to work with owners on a one-off basis. It is tough to put systems and processes as an investor who is also a working professional.

PRIVATE LENDERS

Private lending involves obtaining a loan from a private individual or company, rather than a traditional lender such as a bank. As a new investor with zero experience, I would not try to raise private capital. Here are some drawbacks to working with private lenders as a new investor.

- Barrier to entry: As a new investor working on your very first project, it is tough to find private lenders who trust you with their money and lend to you for your project.

- Private lenders with deep pockets: Not all private lenders are created equal. A lot of private lenders have the ability to fund one deal or a part of a deal. This would mean that you'd be going to a different lender each time you have a deal.

HARD MONEY LENDERS

Hard money lenders are a great way for investors to get started and scale their portfolio. We scaled our portfolio from $0 to $10 million in five years by working primarily with hard money lenders.

Hard money lenders lend money to investors based on the value of the property being purchased. Hard money loans can be approved quickly and provide more flexible terms compared to traditional loans, which can be advantageous for investors who need to include renovation costs in the loan.

Here are some advantages of working with hard money lenders:

- Scalability: Hard money lenders can provide funding for multiple properties at once, which can help investors scale their portfolio more quickly. This is particularly useful for investors using the BRRRR strategy, as they can use the funds from the hard money loan to purchase and renovate multiple properties, and then refinance the properties to pay off the hard money loan.
- Construction inspections: Before any construction draws are approved, hard money lenders typically send their own inspectors to review the renovation work. Their approval is an additional set of eyes ensuring the renovation is on track.

Over the last few years, the short-term lending industry has grown tremendously, providing investors with many options when selecting a hard money lender. The loan term for hard money loans can vary from six months to over a year, depending on the size of the rehab project. Interest rates for the loan can range from 8 to 15 percent. While this may seem like a high interest rate, remember this is a short-term loan. You will include the interest rate in your soft costs when running your numbers, and only proceed with the deal if it makes sense financially. A hard money lender will typically finance a large percentage of the purchase and rehab costs. For example, if the purchase price is $70,000 and the rehab budget is $50,000, the total investment needed is $120,000.

There are hard money lenders who can lend up to 90 percent of the purchase price, and 100 percent of the rehab budget. This means that instead of bringing $120,000 of your own cash to the project, you only bring 10 percent of the purchase price (which, in this example, would be $7,000), and also closing costs, which could be around $10,000. So, the total cash you will bring to the closing table would be $17,000, while the hard money lender will finance the remaining $113,000 ($120,000 − $7,000).

You bring only $17,000 of your own cash instead of $120,000!

(Note: This is just an example, and typically, the more experience you gain, the more favorable the terms become.)

UNDERSTANDING OFFER TO CLOSE COSTS FOR A HARD MONEY LOAN

When it comes to hard money loans, there are a variety of costs associated with the loan process. It's important to have an understanding of these costs so that you can accurately assess the overall expenses of your investment. Below are some of the key costs to consider when looking at an offer to close a hard money loan:

- Appraisal or evaluation fee: A hard money lender will often ask for money to order an appraisal prior to closing.
- Transfer taxes: This is a cost that you will incur at closing.
- Builder's risk insurance: You will have to pay for builder's risk insurance prior to closing, and you'll need to have it ready at closing.
- Title insurance: This is another cost that you will pay at closing, and it will be a part of the closing paperwork and closing costs from the lender.

In addition to these costs, there are several other fees that you should be aware of when working with a hard money lender:

- Origination fee or points: This is a percentage of the loan amount, not the ARV. It will be charged by the lender and can be a significant cost to consider.
- Underwriting fee: This is a charge for underwriting the loan.
- Doc prep fee: This is a charge for drafting loan documents, and it's often paid to a third-party loan processor.
- Processing fee: This is a charge for loan processing.
- Credit report fee: This is a charge for a credit report.
- Wire fee: This is a lender charge paid by the borrower for wire fee from the lender's bank.
- Loan servicing setup fee: Many lenders will have their loans serviced by a third-party loan processing service. This fee is to set that up.
- Legal fees: There might be some legal fees involved in the process.

- Flood certification: This is a charge to verify whether the property is or is not in a flood zone.
- Hold for interest reserves: The lender may hold back six to twelve months of payments, sometimes even three months, to make payments for a specified number of months. This will change what you bring to the table.

It's important to note that hard money lenders do not have a one-size-fits-all formula. The costs can vary depending on several factors, such as the lender, the deal, and your experience. To avoid getting overwhelmed, it's best to pick one lender and get their costs down. This will give you an overall perspective, and you can ask them to quickly go over all their costs.

When it comes to the cash you bring to close a deal, it will also vary depending on the lender, the deal, and your experience. It is important to factor in all the variables before closing a deal.

Now, let's get into the end-to-end life cycle of hard money loans.

END-TO-END LIFE CYCLE FOR HARD MONEY LOANS

Let's take a closer look at the end-to-end life cycle of a hard money loan.

End-to-End Life Cycle for Hard Money Loans

Find the right Hard Money Lender (HML)	HML Application	HML Appraisal	HML Underwriting	HML Closing	HML Construction Draws	Long-term Refinance

Finding the Right HML: The first step in obtaining a hard money loan is to find potential lenders and begin discussions about the terms and conditions of the loan. This may involve researching multiple lenders and populating a lender spreadsheet with their respective terms and rates. It's important to choose reputable lenders who offer competitive terms while requiring the least amount of money from the borrower. This process can take some time and may involve introductory calls and pre-qualifying with the lender to streamline the application process.

HML Application: Once a suitable lender has been identified, it's time for you, the borrower, to prepare a deal packet that includes the necessary documentation and information about the proposed investment property. This packet may include a construction breakdown, rental and ARV comparables, and any other information that the lender may require. It's important to note that some lenders may ask for additional paperwork or conduct a credit check as part of the application process.

HML Appraisal: After the application has been submitted, the next step is the appraisal of the property. The appraisal helps to determine the value of the property and serves as a basis for the loan amount. It's important to involve a title agent at this stage to ensure that all legal requirements are met and to obtain any necessary insurance.

HML Underwriting: After you've completed the appraisal, the loan then goes into underwriting, and you will receive the final terms and conditions. It's at this stage that the lender may require the borrower to obtain builder's risk insurance, which protects against damage or loss during construction. It's important to carefully review all pre-close paperwork and make sure that the terms and conditions are in line with what was discussed earlier in the process.

HML Closing: Prior to the day of closing, the borrower must prepare their share of the funds and may need to wire them in advance or provide a cashier's check. On the day of closing, we suggest you carry a few hundred dollars in cash in case of any unexpected changes. After the loan is closed, the borrower will typically begin to receive construction draws, which are payments made by the lender to cover the costs of construction or renovation.

HML Construction Draws: One of the key benefits of hard money loans for real estate investors is the ability to fund both the purchase and rehab of a property. After the property purchase is funded directly by the lender at closing, the hard money lender will typically provide multiple draws for the rehab portion of the loan, often four draws of 25 percent each. The process for receiving these construction draws involves several steps.

First, the investor must fund the portion of the construction costs not covered by the loan. This typically involves making a deposit to the contractor, as discussed in the rehab module. After the contractor has completed around 25 percent of the work, the investor can submit the necessary paperwork to the hard money lender for an inspection. Once the lender has verified the progress of the construction work, they will wire the draw amount directly to the investor, who can then pay the contractor for the remaining work. It's important to note that the specifics of the construction draw process may vary depending on the lender and the terms of the loan.

Some lenders may require more or fewer draws, while others may have different requirements for documentation or inspections. As with any aspect of hard money lending, it's important to carefully review all terms and conditions and ensure that the lender is reputable and reliable.

One final step in the hard money lending process is to sign a lien waiver. This document confirms that the borrower has paid their contractor in full and prevents the contractor from placing a lien on the property in the future. This is an important step to protect the borrower's investment and ensure a smooth transition to the refinance phase.

In conclusion, the end-to-end life cycle of a hard money loan involves many steps, from identifying potential lenders to preparing a deal packet and securing the loan. While there can be some variability in terms of the time it takes to close a loan, it's important to choose reputable lenders and carefully review all paperwork to ensure a successful outcome. Hard money loans can be a valuable tool for real estate investors, and understanding the process can help to make the most of this type of financing.

The next step is renting out the property (which we covered in the rent chapter) and obtaining long term financing. Let's dive into obtaining long-term commercial financing.

UNLOCKING GROWTH USING LONG-TERM COMMERCIAL FINANCING

After you've completed the rehab stage of the project and your property has been rented to a tenant, you will then start the process of long-term financing.

The option of long-term financing allows you to pay off the hard money lender for the money they brought to the deal, and it allows you to pull out the money you brought to the table. Long-term financing allows you to hold a property for years to come, collecting the cash flow. It allows you to build wealth by covering the mortgage through rent and by paying off the principal.

There are two kinds of loans that you can get for long-term financing—conventional loans or commercial loans. Many new investors use conventional loans when buying an investment property.

Most investors may not use commercial finance for a variety of reasons, including a lack of understanding of the commercial lending process, the perception that commercial lending is too complex, and more comfort with traditional financing options. Shifting from conventional finance to commercial finance can be a beneficial move for investors, particularly those who are looking to build and scale their rental property portfolio.

LIMITATIONS OF CONVENTIONAL LOANS

While conventional loans can be a useful tool for rental property investing, they also come with several limitations and challenges, such as:

- Limitations on the number of loans: Conventional lenders often limit the number of loans that an individual can have, which can make it more difficult for investors to build and scale their rental property portfolio. This is the primary reason we switched to commercial financing.
- Stricter underwriting standards: Conventional lenders typically have stricter underwriting standards compared to other types of lenders, and they tend to require a higher credit score and more extensive documentation. This can make it more difficult for some investors, especially once you become a full-time real estate investor, to qualify for a conventional loan.
- Longer underwriting process: The underwriting process for a conventional loan can take longer compared to other types of loans, which can be a disadvantage for investors who need to move quickly to close a deal.

END-TO-END LIFE CYCLE FOR LONG-TERM COMMERCIAL FINANCING

The long-term commercial financing process can be broken down into several steps, each of which is crucial for success. Here is an overview of the end-to-end life cycle of commercial financing:

End-to-End Life Cycle for Long-Term Commercial Financing

Find the right terms	Application process	Appraisal	Underwriting	Closing

Step 1: Finding the Right Terms

The first step in securing a long-term loan is finding the right terms for your deal. This involves reaching out to lenders and filling up a spreadsheet with their information. Take note of the lenders that best fit your needs, and then move on to the application process.

Step 2: Application Process

Once you have your project underway, it's time to start looking for a permanent loan. Go through the application process with the lender of your choice. They will ask for various documents, including tax returns, credit checks, personal financial statements, and lease agreements. They will also order an appraisal, which will be the first time you will pay them for anything.

Step 3: Appraisal

Long-term Commercial mortgage appraisal is a crucial step, and it requires careful preparation and attention to detail. The goal of the appraisal process is to determine the value of the property, which will be used to calculate the loan amount that the lender is willing to offer. Because there is a lot to cover here, we will discuss this in more detail a bit later in this chapter.

Step 4: Underwriting

The next step is underwriting, which involves requesting stabilized insurance and title company information. You can put the lender in touch with your title company and also get stabilized insurance. Make sure to request the paperwork at least twenty-four hours before closing.

Step 5: Closing

At closing, the lender will give you a check for your cash-out, and they may wire the money if they are doing an E-Close. Make sure to carry a couple of hundred dollars in cash in case any changes occur during closing. You also want to know if they will be escrowing for your taxes and insurance, and if not, make sure to set up those payments along with the mortgage payment.

And now, celebrate!

There are three points in time during a project when you should celebrate: when you close the deal, when you rent it out, and when you refinance it. These are the moments worth celebrating, and they represent the three stages of the BRRRR project. Be grateful for all that you have learned and enjoy owning a property that you worked so hard on.

APPRAISAL

This is one of the most important steps in the process of the supercharged BRRRR strategy.

We set out to run the business of a scattered site portfolio like a CEO with best practices in business. There were no coaches teaching this; however, a good deal of our professional careers had been spent establishing and improving business processes, so we knew we could figure it out.

Creating products with the customer in mind is of paramount importance in business because it ensures that the end product aligns with the needs, wants, and expectations of the target market. By understanding and catering to the needs of the customer, the product will more likely be successful in the marketplace, leading to increased revenue and profitability for the company. In other words, creating products with the customer in mind enables a company to create products that will sell, ultimately leading to the financial success of the business.

In the case of a real estate investing business with the buy and hold strategy, the product would be a rental unit. So it makes sense that we would create a product that was comfortable and competitive in the eyes of the tenant.

However, in the BRRRR strategy, the refinance stage can determine whether we can cash-out all of the money that has been invested in the deal. This would rely on what the After Repair Value of the property ends up being once an appraisal is done. If you think about it, the property isn't being renovated just to please the tenant. The property is also being renovated with one additional customer in mind: the appraiser. Granted, the appraiser really isn't a real estate investor's customer, but in this context, treating the appraiser like a customer has allowed us to consistently achieve higher valuations for our properties.

As a real estate investor, establishing a good relationship with an appraiser can be beneficial in a number of ways. Some steps you can take to establish a good relationship with an appraiser include:

Build Trust: Appraisers rely on accurate and complete information to make their determinations. By providing them with all the necessary information, you can establish trust and build a rapport. More on this in a bit.

Communicate Clearly and Be Responsive: Respond to the appraiser's requests for information and follow up on any questions they may have in a timely manner.

Respect Their Professionalism: Appraisers are trained professionals, and they have their own process of doing their work. Respect their expertise and the work they do.

Here are some ideas for the type of information you can provide.

- Property description: A detailed description of the property including square footage, number of bedrooms and bathrooms, age of the property, and any unique features or amenities, including any recent renovations or upgrades that have been made to the property.
- Property photos: High-quality photographs of the property, including exterior, interior, and any special features or amenities, as well as before and after pictures of any renovations or upgrades.
- Property information sheet: A document that includes the property address, legal description, zoning, and any recent sales or property value history, as well as the current market rent for the property and any lease agreements.
- Property maps: Maps showing the property location, boundaries, and surrounding area, as well as any nearby amenities or public transportation.
- Title report: A document that includes information about the property's title and any liens or encumbrances on the property, as well as any recent title changes or transactions.
- Home inspection report: A report detailing any issues or repairs that need to be made to the property, as well as any recent repairs or upgrades that have been made.
- Appraisal report: A report from a previous appraiser, if available, as well as any recent comps that have been done on the property.
- List of comparable properties: A list of similar properties in the area that have recently sold or are currently on the market, as well as any properties that have been recently refinanced.
- Other relevant documents: Any other documents that may be relevant to the property, such as building permits or zoning variances, as well as any recent financial statements or tax returns.
- Contact information: The contact information for the property owner or listing agent, as well as any other relevant parties, such as the current mortgage lender or refinancing lender.

LLC OR NOT TO LLC

We are often asked this question about whether one should invest under an LLC or their personal name. Working with an LLC (Limited Liability Company) can provide several advantages for investors who are acquiring rental properties for BRRRR using hard money and commercial financing. These advantages include:

Liability Protection: An LLC can give you a level of protecting to your personal assets from any legal or financial liability that may arise from your rental property investments.

Access to Hard Money to Fund Purchase and Rehab: Most hard money lenders require you to purchase the asset under an LLC.

Access to Long-term Commercial Financing: Most long-term commercial lenders require you to purchase the asset under an LLC.

SYSTEMS

Shareable Google Sheets for Personal Financial Statement and Schedule of Properties

Most commercial lenders will require you to provide these two documents as part of their process. Usually, lenders will provide their own template that you are required to complete. These templates vary only slightly by lender but are tedious to fill out. A great hack is to create your own template in Google Sheets and share it lenders using a view-only link.

To create a personal financial statement, you will need to gather information about your assets, liabilities, and net worth. This will include information about your bank account balances, investments, real estate holdings, and personal residence. You will also need to provide information about your annual income, expenses, and debt payments (e.g., mortgage, car loans, etc.).

Once you have a complete personal financial statement, you can use it to apply for financing with commercial lenders. You can also use it as a tool to track your progress over time and make informed decisions about your rental portfolio.

Creating a schedule of properties is another important step in securing financing for your commercial properties. This document lists all of the properties that you own, along with relevant information such as the property address, purchase price, current value, and any rental income that you receive.

By creating a schedule of properties, you can provide commercial lenders with a clear picture of your rental portfolio and demonstrate that you have a solid investment strategy. This can help you secure better financing terms and position you for success in the rental property market.

DOCUMENT MANAGEMENT SYSTEM

A Document Management System is the process of organizing, storing, and tracking documents in a way that makes them easy to access and use. As a rental property investor, you will accumulate a lot of documents over time, including lease agreements, property inspection reports, insurance policies, tax records, and more. Effective document management involves creating a system for organizing and storing all of these documents so that you can easily find what you need when you need it.

A few decades ago, this involved setting up physical filing systems. Nowadays, with digital storage solutions like cloud-based storage or document management software, it has become incredibly easy and efficient. You can even send documents within seconds right from your smartphone while you're with your kids at the playground, as soon as a lender requests them. This establishes a streamlined relationship.

Here are a few tips for using Google Drive to create your own Document Management System:

- Create a new folder specifically for each property labeling them by their addresses or names, and within each, create sub-folders for various steps. For example, "Finance."
- Upload all relevant documents for each property into its corresponding subfolder on an ongoing basis. Useful tools (the notes app on your phone and other apps, such as Genius scan) eliminate the need to purchase a scanner and be able to scan documents on the go so you can maintain your Document Management System.
- Examples of documents to include might be purchase agreements, leases, property tax records, insurance policies, inspection reports, and appraisals.
- Make sure all documents are properly labeled and organized so you can quickly find what you need when you need it.
- Set permissions for each folder and subfolder to ensure they're only accessible to authorized users.
- Share the link to the specific folder or subfolder containing the required documents with the lender or anyone else who needs to access them.

By following these steps, you can easily manage and organize all necessary documents for your rental property investment portfolio in one secure location, making it easy to quickly access and share information with lenders and other relevant parties.

PROCESSES

ANNUAL RETURN ON EQUITY CALCULATION

To scale your rental portfolio quickly, it's crucial to understand the concept of Return on Equity (ROE). Investors talk a lot about Return in Investment (ROI), which is certainly important, but many of them overlook it. ROE is a metric that measures the return you are earning on the equity you have in a property.

As we discussed earlier in this book, equity in a property is calculated by subtracting the loan amount on the property from the current market value of the property. So, for example, the current market value of your property is $150,000, and the mortgage on it is 75 percent, which is $112,500. This means that your equity in the property is $37,500 ($150,000 − $112,500). And say your annual cash flow on the property is $3,600. (Remember, cash flow is calculated by deducting mortgage payments and expenses from your rent.)

In this scenario, your **ROE is 9.8 percent** ($3,600 / $37,500).

Now, over the next five years, the property is likely to appreciate. Let's say the property appreciates to $180,000 in five years. Since you have a long-term mortgage on the property, your loan amount of $112,500 stays the same. But because of the appreciation, your equity in the property is now $67,500 ($180,000 − $112,500). And let's assume that your cash flow increases from $3,600 to $4,000 over the five years.

Now, your **ROE is 5.9 percent.** This is because as your equity in the property increases, your cash flow may not increase at the same rate.

In other words, the more equity you have in the property, the lower your returns are likely to be relative to the equity.

That is why it is very important to harvest that equity from time to time in order to increase your returns. You can harvest your equity in two ways:

1. Do another cash-out refinance: You can do a cash-out refinance to tap into the equity, and then use that cash to invest in another property. We typically do this for each of our properties every two to three years for each of our properties.
2. Sell your property: Alternatively, you can sell the property and use

the funds to buy another larger property. 1031 exchange is a great way to defer taxes from your gains by buying another property.

By regularly analyzing your ROE and making informed decisions about your investments, you can scale your portfolio a lot faster!

PAPERLESS BACK-OFFICE

As an engineer, I (Palak) helped various organizations go paperless. This involved working with scanning companies to digitize thousands of drawings and papers, resulting in incredible cost savings and increased savings.

When we started investing in rentals, I realized that document management was going to be critical and started implementing the same systems within my own business. Going paperless as a real estate investor offers several benefits, including:

Increased Efficiency: Digital documents can be accessed quickly and easily, reducing the time spent searching through physical files. With a paperless system, you can quickly search, sort, and organize files, making it easier to find the information you need when you need it.

Improved Organization: Digital documents can be sorted, labeled, and filed in a way that is much easier and faster than their physical counterparts. This means you can keep your files better organized and find the information you need more quickly, without having to sift through piles of paper.

Reduced Clutter: By going paperless, you can significantly reduce the amount of clutter in your workspace. This can help you stay focused and productive, making it easier to find the documents you need.

Lower Costs: Printing and storing physical documents can be costly, and going paperless can help reduce these expenses. You won't need to purchase as much paper or printer ink, and you won't need to pay for as much storage space.

Environmental Benefits: Going paperless can also have a positive impact on the environment. By reducing the amount of paper you use, you can help conserve natural resources and reduce the amount of waste sent to landfills.

Some tools essential for this are:

- Fujitsu Scansnap 500: This scanner isn't cheap, but it is an investment that will allow you to scan a large pile of documents quickly and accurately.

- Virtual Mailbox: There are many on the market like Anytime Mailbox and Earth Class Mail. Make sure you vet these companies for how they do a background check on their employees.
- Google Drive App for the Phone: The drive app has come a long way and can be very useful when sharing documents on the go.
- Notes App: If you are required to sign a document, you can import it into the notes app and sign with your finger. It removes the need for printing, signing, scanning, and emailing.
- Shredder or Shredding Service: We use a service called Shred-it that offers on-site pickup for documents that need to be shredded. You can also invest in a shredder if you do not want to use a service. Some shredders are incredible heavy and not easy to use. Be sure to try them at a store prior to ordering them online.

TEAMS

HML INSPECTOR

As a rental property investor, working with a hard money lender's inspector can be a valuable resource to help keep tabs on your contractor and ensure that your project stays on track. Here are some steps you can take to leverage this resource effectively:

Communicate with your hard money lender's inspector. Once your HML has assigned an inspector to your project, establish clear lines of communication with the inspector. Let them know about your project, what you hope to accomplish, and the timeline you are working under. Make sure the inspector has all of the relevant details and contact information for you and your contractor.

Schedule regular inspections. Work with your inspector to schedule regular inspections at key points in your project's timeline. This will help you stay on track and ensure that your contractor is meeting the necessary milestones. By having a third-party inspector on hand, you can get an unbiased assessment of the quality of the work being done and identify any potential issues early on.

Be present during inspections (physically or virtually). It's important to be available during (or right after) inspections so that you can discuss any issues or concerns with your inspector and your contractor. This will also give you an opportunity to see the progress being made and make any necessary adjustments to the project.

COMMERCIAL PORTFOLIO LENDERS

Commercial portfolio lenders are a great option for real estate investors looking to finance their properties. Portfolio lenders typically hold on to their loans in-house, giving them more flexibility in their underwriting guidelines and can make loan decisions based on a more holistic approach, including the borrower's overall financial situation and the specific property being financed. Portfolio lenders may also have quicker turnaround times and can offer more customized loan terms. These lenders can be a great resource for real estate investors looking for flexible, customized financing options.

ACE UP THE SLEEVE—DSCR LENDERS

We often hear form investors who don't have a W-2 job (either because they own a small business, or because they are transitioning to full-time investing) that they find it difficult to obtain a long-term loan on their rentals.

When Palak quit her job, we became a single-income family and lost half of our household income. This negatively impacted our debt-to-income (DTI) ratio, which measures the percentage of a borrower's income that is used to pay their monthly debts. Most traditional lenders, including banks, consider DTI as a criteria when assessing a borrower's eligibility for a loan. We were worried that this would impact our ability to scale our portfolio.

Then, we discovered DSCR loans. DSCR stands for Debt Service Coverage Ratio, and DSCR loans are a type of commercial loan that takes into account the borrower's ability to make loan payments based on their property's income, not just your personal income. The higher the DSCR, the more cash flow the property generates to cover the loan payments, which increases the likelihood of loan approval.

Another big advantage of DSCR loans is scalability. There is no limit to how many DSCR loans you can obtain, as long as you are investing in positive cash-flowing rentals. This makes DSCR loans an ace up the sleeve for investors looking to scale their portfolio.

MEET ROCKSTAR INVESTOR CATHY

Cathy used to work a regular nine-to-five job. She wanted to invest in real estate but didn't have a clear plan. As a working mom who wanted to take action and do more for her family, Cathy needed knowledge and a push in the right direction.

Why?

Cathy admitted to not having the necessary information about the industry to create her own creative financing plan. Like many of us, Cathy was raised thinking that all debt was bad debt, and she was reluctant to borrow. This held her back from unlocking the full potential of real estate investing.

Let's look at some of Cathy's results once she learned the strategy and the tactics and surrounded herself with like-minded investors.

One of her recent deals was a single-family unit in Tulsa, Oklahoma. It had a purchase price of $56,000. This was a wholesale deal with a projected $40,000 in rehab. Even in the worst-case scenario, her ARV is calculated in the $130,000 to $135,000, which would generate her $35,000 in equity.

But that's not the most exciting result.

Within six months, Cathy had two LLCs, one located in Arkansas and another in Oklahoma. She's never felt more confident as an investor, and she can see a clear path of success in front of her moving forward.

CHAPTER NINE
Exponential Growth (Repeat)

We have already talked about how to set up your business to scale from the beginning using the SCALE strategy. However, we have discovered over time that there are a few additional elements that can help increase your growth and significantly reduce your time to financial freedom. In this chapter, we will explore how to scale exponentially with the key philosophical, mindset, strategic and tactical shifts that we have implemented over the years and seen massive results each time.

THE 80/20 RULE

You've probably heard of the 80/20 Rule, also known as the Pareto Principle. Italian economist Vilfredo Pareto observed that 80 percent of Italy's land was owned by 20 percent of the population. He then found similar distributions in various other countries he surveyed. Since then, this principle has been successfully applied to sports, taxation, software, health, and more. It wasn't until we started our entrepreneurship journey that we learned how versatile this principle is, including how it can be used for prioritization of tasks.

To an entrepreneur, all tasks can seem urgent and have direct financial implications. It's easy to get into the "whack-a-mole" mindset, existing in a state of constant fire drills. We applied the 80/20 lens to the business of real estate investing to see how it could help. Lo and behold, we discovered that 20 percent of the tasks that we performed generated 80 percent of our revenue. Applying this principle allowed us to save time, increase profitability, and savings.

APPLICATION OF THE 80/20 RULE

We tried multiple methods to tackle a pare down of the never-ending list of to-dos. One of them included tracking all the tasks performed for a month including the easy/mundane ones that occupied brain space. However, that method was exhausting and stressful, adding an extra task each time we performed to our already long list of to-dos. Then we found a solution.

STRATEGY: REDUCE THE NUMBER OF WORKING HOURS

Most of us who have a steady paycheck want to invest in real estate long-term so we can build wealth and earn passive income to win our time back. Keeping that goal as the North Star, the key to finding the 20 percent of the tasks that provide 80 percent of the output, consider working no more than five hours per day. And then reduce it further once that feels comfortable. We found that we were automatically forced to pare down the to-do list due to the limited time.

We also started doing a "time versus money" analysis to determine which tasks were worth our time and which ones could be eliminated or outsourced. This analysis involves calculating the dollar amount associated with a task and the number of hours it takes to complete it.

However, we were still trying to be extremely productive by doing almost the same amount of work (even after being pared down) in a shorter amount of time, which defeats the purpose of reducing working hours in the first place.

TACTIC: THEME YOUR DAYS

Finally, when we implemented a powerful tactic, we were able to figure a way to improve our productivity. That tactic was to theme our days. This concept has been around for a while and involves batching similar work together on a single day. It is a simple but powerful method that can provide significant benefits.

For instance, you can block Mondays for marketing, Tuesdays for accounting, Thursdays for site visits, and so on. The two most obvious advantages of theming days are, first, that it establishes focus and attention, getting us out of the "whack-a-mole" mindset. Second, by grouping similar tasks together, we can complete them much faster and more efficiently.

For example, when we were driving up to visit rehab projects every day, we realized that previously, as salaried employees, we weren't sufficiently trained to think about the value of time. When we started to theme our days, we strictly "forbade" ourselves from visiting the jobsites on the days designated for other themes. Using a FaceTime/WhatsApp video call as opposed to physically visiting the jobsites every single day saved us about five hours per week. We eventually reduced site visits to once a week, which was more than sufficient since we had a trustworthy and competent crew. After a few months, we even moved over to completely virtual project management. if you're not comfortable with this idea just yet, consider hiring an assistant who can do weekly jobsite visits and provide detailed photos and videos. This is just one example of the endless possibilities of themed days!

MINDSET SHIFT: LET GO OF THE NEED FOR PERFECTION

The third and the biggest advantage of implementing the lower working hours and themed days to get closer to 80/20 was in the intangibles. Before this strategy, we couldn't see the forest for the trees. After implementing it, we felt more present and can think even bigger!

In Hal Elrod's book *The Miracle Morning*, Jim Rohn is quoted as saying, "Your level of success will rarely exceed your level of personal development, because success is something you attract by the person you become." We couldn't agree more.

If the idea of the 80/20 rule brings up some uncomfortable feelings, it is due to the years of conditioning that has stopped you from exploring your higher potential. Welcome this uncomfortable feeling, sit with it, and let whatever comes up, come up.

When asked to describe themselves, many of the folks we work with will use the words "independent," "passionate," and, more often than not, "perfectionist." Perhaps you can relate. They have a thriving career, great family and friends, and are generally happy. Yet, something is missing. They find themselves wondering if they were meant to do big things, if there's more to their potential they could explore. However, despite this nagging feeling, they feel stuck.

These attributes that people tend to use when they describe themselves typically showcase their strengths.

However, it's time to start looking at them as drawbacks.

These positive attributes allow us to achieve growth and progress. They allow us to be liked by our employers and customers and have great relationships with friends and family. But that's the problem, you see! These are the same qualities that stop us from becoming the best we can be, to tap into our fullest potential. By being the detail-oriented person that everyone expects us to be, we miss out on becoming the powerful people we are meant to be—the ones that run large empires, the ones people look up to.

Do you know the two biggest differences between "perfectionist" and "powerful"? Delegation and outsourcing.

Let go of that control and trying to deliver the product perfectly. It's not your job. Your job is to move mountains, build companies the size of kingdoms, and focus on changing the world. Get out of that comfort zone and grow with strategic partnerships and bringing the right people to do the right tasks. Because no successful entrepreneur ever has said, "I wish I had worked in my business as opposed to on my business!"

We'll explore how to build a robust team of people you can count on in the next chapter.

GROW BEFORE PAYING OFF

Using debt to purchase assets is a common practice among wealthy individuals and experienced real estate investors. The reason behind this is simple: debt allows individuals to purchase more assets than they could otherwise afford with their own cash. In other words, debt helps to magnify investment returns, and this can result in higher long-term wealth creation.

However, many new real estate investors are often hesitant to use leverage due to fear of potential financial losses or due to a lack of understanding about how to use it effectively. However, it is important for these individuals to get over this fear and embrace the power of leverage.

One of the biggest advantages of using leverage is that it enables new real estate investors to make more money with less money. Leveraging increases buying power, allowing individuals to purchase more assets than they would be able to with their own cash. Additionally, leveraging can help to reduce the overall risk of an investment portfolio. This is because a portfolio of assets purchased with debt is typically more diversified, which helps to spread risk and minimize potential losses.

Finally, leveraging can also help to maximize tax benefits. This is because the interest payments on debt used to purchase assets are tax-deductible, which can help to reduce the overall cost of ownership.

Leveraging is a powerful tool that can help to maximize investment returns and, counter-intuitively, reduce risk. By overcoming their fear of using leverage, new real estate investors can open up new opportunities and increase their wealth creation potential.

Once assets are acquired through debt, they have the potential to generate income, which can be used to pay down the debt and build equity. This creates a positive feedback loop, where assets generate more income, which can then be used to acquire more assets. Over time, this process can lead to a significant increase in wealth.

The reverse, however, is another story. Without assets, it can be challenging to generate significant cash flow to invest in new assets. This is because income streams are typically limited, and it can be difficult to scale up a business or investment portfolio without significant assets to begin with.

This is why many successful investors and entrepreneurs focus on building assets before focusing on increasing their cash flow. By doing so, they create a foundation of wealth that can then be leveraged to create even more wealth over time.

Building assets through leveraging can be a powerful strategy for creating long-term wealth. By focusing on acquiring assets first, individuals can establish a foundation of wealth that can be leveraged to create more income and grow their investment portfolios. This can be much more difficult to do without assets, as it can be challenging to generate significant cash flow without a foundation of wealth to build upon.

ACCELERATE SCALE BY FINDING MORE SEED MONEY

When following the SCALE strategy, each property you acquire can be a stepping stone toward financial freedom. you will find that each property is a ray of light leading you toward financial freedom. With each property you BRRRR, you gain the potential to generate more assets over time. This can even be doubled or tripled if you can find more seed money. So, let's talk about sources of capital that can accelerate your journey to financial freedom.

Limited capital is the primary obstacle new investors find it difficult to scale. We wanted to avoid knocking on the doors of private lenders or exploring partnerships. Although the strategy does allow one to pull out funds and recycle them, having additional funds to start multiple projects at the same time can exponentially fast track your success.

To keep growing our real estate portfolio, we had to find more capital. We did it using a variety of ways. Here are some ideas:

HELOC/HOME EQUITY LOANS ON PRIMARY RESIDENCE

One of the most powerful ways you can do this is by leveraging a home equity line of credit (HELOC) on your primary residence. In one year, we grew our portfolio from three to twenty properties by turbo-charging the BRRRR strategy with home equity loans.

WHAT IS A HOME EQUITY LOAN?

If you've owned your primary residence for a few years, chances are you've built up equity in the property. There are three ways to tap into this equity: selling the property, doing a cash-out refinance, or borrowing against the equity.

If you have a good interest rate locked in, you may not want to sell or do a cash-out refinance. In this case, exploring home equity loans is a viable option.

This strategy doesn't require selling your primary residence or refinancing the existing mortgage on it. Instead, you're borrowing against the property, tapping into its equity. After using this as capital to fund a deal, we would go through the BRRRR process, and after refinancing the rental property, we would pay off the HELOC and then repeat the same process for the next rental property.

ADVANTAGES OF HOME EQUITY LOANS AND HELOCS

There are certainly advantages to utilizing these borrowing options, including:

Interest rates for such loans are significantly lower than credit card interest rates. I've seen some aggressive fellow investors use personal credit cards for down payments for their BRRRR strategy. There are much lower risk options.

HELOC is looked at more favorably by banks than personal credit card debt, giving you a higher chance of getting approved for permanent loans in the future. Most importantly, you can keep an existing property, furthering your portfolio by avoiding selling.

WHAT TO KEEP IN MIND WHEN USING A HELOC

Would using this strategy mean that you'd be more leveraged? Absolutely! It goes without saying that the deals that you do (especially in the market cycle we are in) need to be not just good deals—but great.

Here are a couple of things to keep in mind:

- Your debt-to-income ratio (DTI) takes a hit. When you borrow money in your own name, your debt-to-income ratio goes up. If you borrow money under an LLC but personally guarantee it, your global DTI comes into play. It is harder for banks to give you permanent financing when they see that your DTI doesn't meet their standards. So, it's best to only take on an amount of debt that will keep your DTI at a good level.

- It requires discipline to not use money from HELOC to make other purchases. Focus on furthering your portfolio.

401(K)

One strategy we used early on when we both had W-2 jobs to obtain capital for seed money was to borrow from our 401(k) to invest in real estate. Whether it's a good idea or not depends on your specific financial situation, risk tolerance, and investment goals. We saw tremendous opportunity in being able to access the funds to further our real estate portfolio because of two primary benefits:

1. When you borrow from your 401(k), the interest rate you pay on the loan is usually lower than what you would pay for a credit card.
2. You are not technically withdrawing funds from your 401(k) account, so you can avoid the early withdrawal penalty that would normally apply to withdrawals made before age fifty-nine and a half.

If you want to borrow money against your 401(k) plan, you will need to check with your plan administrator to see if it allows for loans. Not all 401(k) plans offer loan options, and even those that do may have specific rules and limitations. Assuming your 401(k) plan does allow for loans, you can generally borrow up to 50 percent of your vested account balance. There may also be limits to the dollar amount you can borrow.

TAX RETURNS

I (Niti) affectionately make fun of Palak because I could never love tax time as much as she does. When we had our W-2 jobs and first moved in together, she used to take a lot of pride and joy in gathering documents and filing taxes. I then realized why she was so excited. She paid additional in taxes each month and expected a big return at the end. If you want to receive a large tax refund each year to use as a force savings for real estate investing, you can adjust your tax withholding by submitting a new Form W-4 to your employer. The W-4 is used to determine how much income tax is withheld from your paycheck. Determine the additional amount of tax withholding you need to have taken out of your paycheck each pay period. Fill out a new Form W-4 with your employer and provide the additional withholding amount.

This tip may go against what many financial advisors suggest. While receiving a large tax refund may provide a force savings for real estate investing, it also means that you are giving the government an interest-free loan for the year. However, we decided to go against this advice because the interest we'd make on those savings would be so minimal that we did not mind lending the government a bit of money interest-free if it forced us to save.

Some advisors might also say that it is more beneficial to invest the additional money throughout the year to earn interest and potentially achieve a higher return. However, this advice does not take human nature into account. Out of sight is out of mind. Not seeing that money is the best way to save it for a lot of us. Just remember to re-deploy it as seed money for your SCALE property.

SCALING WITH SMALL MULTIFAMILY

There are many amazing benefits of starting with the 3S Framework and with single-family homes. However, at a certain point, it may be beneficial to scale faster using small multifamily properties. We recommend doing this once single-family projects feel comfortable and streamlined. When deciding whether to BRRRR a single-family home or a small multifamily property, there are several factors to consider:

Higher cash flow: A multifamily property may generate more rental income than a single-family home, resulting in higher cash flow.

Financing: Small multifamily properties can generate more cash flow, making it easier to secure financing.

Market demand: While the overall cash flow and total rent generated for a multifamily home may be higher than a single-family home in the same area, the individual units might rent for cheaper than a single-family home, making them easier to rent.

AUTOMATE, ELIMINATE, DELEGATE, DO

We wanted to share a great framework you can implement right away to take work off your plate. Create a table of repeatable tasks as you go through your first project and then divide them into four areas. Think about what you can:

1. Automate
2. Eliminate
3. Delegate
4. Do

As an engineer, Palak's brain immediately thinks of automating any task that she finds. As a property manager, she created a series of emails that would seamlessly take tenants through their onboarding process. She included a Google form on our website that our handyman could use with a simple link to fill out using their smartphone during move-in walk-throughs with tenants.

As someone who worked in strategy for the majority of my career, I (Niti) excel at eliminating tasks. So, when I joined the real estate business full time, I created a flow chart of the property management process and eliminated over 40 percent of the tasks.

Next is delegation. Consider adding a virtual assistant to your team. Our in-house property management team consisted of both a virtual assistant and a handyman. Together, they were able to run things seamlessly.

Last, keeps things like deal analysis and finance under the "do" list. As CEO of a thriving real estate investing business, you want to stay informed about your acquisitions and bank relationships.

RESPONSIBILITY VERSUS AUTHORITY

It's not enough to simply give someone responsibility for a task. There are many instances in which your team may not be able to accomplish something because they lack the necessary authority. Think of authority along the same lines of freedom here because the two concepts overlap.

The end goal of delegating a task to someone is to have them finish it and achieve the desired results. However, must be some room for flexibility. Give your team the authority to complete a task in whatever way they deem most efficient.

You provide your team with authority and trust them to come up with ideas on how to do things more efficiently. This will always work toward your advantage, as long as you make one thing clear: they should deliver the results you specified, even if they decide to alter the manner in which a task is handled.

This is exactly what happened when we allowed our contractor to choose the finishes for rehab projects and purchase materials for each rehab. The finishes weren't to our own taste, we'll admit. However, contrary to what HGTV shows may lead us to believe, design is a very small element of true wealth building through the power of long-term buy-and-holds with BRRRR.

Asking our contractor to purchase material and pick finishes for our projects turned out to be one of the single most time-and cost-saving decisions we've made. It turns out that he actually enjoyed it more because he had more independence, got to be more creative, and didn't need to coordinate with us. Additionally, he gets better prices than we do because of his connections with suppliers. This saves us a few hours a week that we would spend shopping around for the best prices on all materials we purchase, keeping track of the schedule, and all the paperwork that went along with this. Overall, by being relatively hands-off on rehabs and outsourcing the material purchase and finishes to the contractor, we saved about eight hours per week and about 10 percent on our overall project costs. Moreover, it allows our contractor to take a lot of pride in his work—which is an unexpected benefit.

That said, there must be checks and balances in place. In this case, we provide a list of finishes to the contractor. For example, where to buy the countertop is up to him, but we are specific about the material, such as granite level 1, and in some instances, a color scheme as well. You can download a list of finishes we use at www.biggerpockets.com/acceleratebonus.

CHOOSE THE RIGHT PEOPLE FOR THE JOB

One of the first lessons for investors who want to operate their real estate investing like a business is to come to terms with their strengths and weaknesses, and to be 100 percent honest with themselves about it. It's important to understand what you can do better than anyone else, and to recognize what others do better than you.

Hiring people with the right skills and delegating the right tasks to the most qualified individuals is key to increasing overall efficiency. An ideal candidate would have the ability to take a task off your plate, be self-motivated, and be good at their job.

Take some time to identify the strengths and weaknesses of potential team members, and be willing to pay top dollar for the right team member. Remember, the right person or the right job is worth the time it takes to find them.

FOCUS ON CLEAR COMMUNICATION

Be very upfront about what you want. Get clear on timelines, deliverables, and resources your team members might need to accomplish your goals. This will ensure that everyone can recheck what was assigned to them, refresh their memory of the instructions, and do it all without reaching out to you consistently for help and guidance. Give people directions and do so as clearly as you can if you want to set your team up for success.

Last, be sure to communicate with tools that the end user can easily access. For example, trying to get a contractor who you need at the jobsite to view instructions using a tool that requires complicated technology use is impractical.

FEEDBACK

The secret to continuously improving your relationship with your team is to monitor progress in a way that isn't overbearing as well as provide and accept constructive feedback. Check in with your team occasionally to see if your instructions are helpful or if they need more direction. Ask your team if they have ideas about streamlining processes that would make their lives easier.

Ideas for language you can use to check in with your team include: "How can I help you do your job better?" or "My job is to help you do your job. What can we do better next time?"

Something we always like to state first when we start doing business with someone if applicable is, "Let's treat this project as a trial. Once we are done, we can go over what worked and what didn't work so we can cultivate a long-term relationship."

CLARITY IS CRITICAL

Any project you post will require a description. In some cases, you may not even need to specify the exact amount until after accepting some bids. However, the project description is vital.

If you want people or companies to bid on your projects, they need to understand what you expect them to do. A lack of details could make people hesitant to contact you, and it could also put you in touch with the wrong people and you'll end up wasting time—the exact opposite of the reason you decided to outsource.

Clear communication will help you get in touch with the likeliest individuals and businesses that can complete your projects in promptly and meet your goals.

STAY AWAY FROM THE LOWEST BIDS

It's incredibly tempting to want to save money by outsourcing work to the cheapest freelancers, but it's important to remember that there's a pecking order in this line of work. The better someone is, the more they can afford to charge. The lowest bids can be dirt cheap for a number of reasons. Someone could be trying to scam you. That person may lack experience and is willing to work for less to learn—which may not be of interest to you.

Although outsourcing is supposed to save time and increase profitability, it shouldn't create a debate about quality and price. For outsourcing to work in your favor, the work you receive should be up to your standards. So, take some time and evaluate different bids and quotes instead of letting prices mislead you. Of course, this also cuts both ways, as not all premium bids are all they're cracked up to be.

ESTABLISH LONG-TERM RELATIONSHIPS

The type of work that you can outsource rarely involves one-and-done projects. Instead, it usually consists of repetitive tasks or projects that you'll need to complete in your business in the future. These tasks may be low value, but they are still important. To save yourself even more time in the long run, it's best to engage in long-term outsourcing projects where only one freelancer or company takes care of your recurring needs. This way, you won't have to keep searching for new people to take on some of your tasks on a weekly or monthly basis.

Furthermore, the more someone works with you, the more opportunities they have for growth. They'll become more efficient at doing the work you need in the way you want it done, and they'll be able to achieve the desired results more quickly.

If you're looking to save a few bucks, keep in mind that long-term projects might get you a discount for repeat business. Additionally, these projects may even help you establish new connections that you can leverage in the future for different tasks.

BUILDING A BANK OF STANDARD OPERATING PROCEDURES

As you build and scale your portfolio, consider starting an SOP bank. A standard operating procedure (SOP) is a set of written instructions that document a step-by-step process to accomplish a specific task that is to be followed by members of an organization. Standard operating procedures are essential parts of good quality systems. Sound and well-written SOPs enhance consistency and reduce human error. If you are just starting out, build an SOP bank using simpler, informal tools first and then transition to more complex applications.

We started writing out our SOPs in Trello with simple, step-by-step informal written processes at first. After a few iterations, we moved them over to Google Docs. If you're growing your portfolio quickly and want transition to more interactive tools, Asana, Click Up, Notion, or other similar applications are great options.

The key is to choose an option that will be sustainable in the long term, easy to share, edit, and protect, and, most importantly, in case of change in team members, give you comfort knowing that most new team members can quickly and easily pick up the application.

SCALING WITH CONFIDENCE IN AN UNCERTAIN MARKET

The world of SCALE-ing with BRRRR is rewarding and exciting, but uncertainties can make new investors feel wary. However, with the right mindset and strategies in place, you can confidently scale your investments even in an uncertain market.

FOCUS ON LONG-TERM SUCCESS

Real estate is a long-term game, and when scaling your investments, the right perspective matters. Instead of focusing on strategies that provide short-term gain, focus on building a sustainable and profitable portfolio, even if it takes time. By investing in cash-flowing assets, you can create a solid foundation for long-term real estate success. The best time to plant a tree was ten years ago; the second-best time is now. And the same goes with buying real estate. As the often-referenced saying goes, it is not about timing the market, it is about time in the market. Wealth creation happens when we hold assets for a long period of time.

OPPORTUNITY AND CONTROL

Market fluctuations can be unsettling, but they also come with opportunities for savvy investors who are willing to adapt. Learn to spot the opportunities and don't let fear paralyze you.

Focus on the things you can control, and learn to pull the levers in your analysis. When one lever goes down, the other one can be pulled.

Here are some examples we have seen firsthand.

- When interest rates are high (which, as we write this book, they are), you may think your deals may not cash flow. But this is an opportunity to find great deals. Because the BRRRR strategy is so forgiving, you can snag good deals now and always RE-refinance the property again in a few years when the interest rates are lower. If it's a good deal with a high interest rate, it's only going to be

better if you can snag a lower rate further down the line—just don't rely on it in the short term when you're crunching your numbers.
- When property values are high, it may seem like deals are hard to find. However, higher property values mean higher ARVs can during the Refinance phase of BRRRR.
- During economic downturns, the equity in your property may go down—but you will still cash flow. Plus, during tougher markets, sellers may be more prone to negotiate on price or terms.

STAY INFORMED AND EDUCATED

Staying informed and educated can help you navigate unfamiliar market conditions. Real estate is a life-long learning game. Continue investing in yourself so you can stay informed about changes that may impact your investing plans.

You can listen to our video on investing with confidence in an uncertain market and download the ebook that goes with it at www.biggerpockets.com/acceleratebonus.

MEET ROCKSTAR INVESTOR ANGELA

Angela had been in the real estate industry for about six years. Six years prior, she had been a burned-out teacher and had made the switch to real estate to escape the grind and create wealth and passive income.

Angela started out as a real estate agent instead of an investor because that seemed like a good first step. However, well-meaning advisors can derail many aspiring investors from their original goals. This was the case with Angela. Six years later, Angela had still not invested in real estate. The skills she acquired as an agent did not directly translate to investing. She was not unhappy about her growth as a real estate agent, but she was still immersed in an active business, one that meant trading hours for dollars. She saw other investors spend their days at the jobsite, Home Depot, doing their own bookkeeping and answering their own phone calls. She wondered if it was going to work out for her as an investor with two little kids and a thriving business as an agent. She simply did not have the time to do it all herself.

Angela still wanted to become an investor but realized she needed a push, education, and a supportive community to make the transition. But more than any of that, she needed a new philosophy on how to do it in 20 percent of the time it took other investors to do it.

Today, Angela has a multi-million-dollar portfolio all thanks to this strategy, but more importantly, she does it with very little time commitment due to the method of execution that is very specific to the type of investor she wanted to be.

Along with education, sharing experiences, working with people who have done it before, and having accountability, were what Angela needed to make the transition. Being surrounded by like-minded investors chasing the same goals and taking those first steps helped Angela to see the domino effect that's possible in real estate investment.

She no longer feels held back by anything when it comes to pursuing her dream and becoming a successful investor. Angela has the blueprint, the strategy, and most importantly, the method of execution to pursue deal after deal.

CHAPTER TEN

Taking Action with the Able Framework

When we first started, we had to guess whether something holding us back was a unique mindset shift we needed to make because of our background or circumstances, or whether it was a recurring issue within the industry for majority of new investors. This led us to consume as much content as we could get our hands on. It wasn't until we learned that it's not about how much information we consume, but what consume that we started making progress.

While they say that knowledge is power, it can become a hinderance to success when there is too much of it. We live in an information-overloaded world. We listen to hundreds of podcasts and read numerous stories about how people started in real estate in different ways, and we wonder, "Am I on the right path?" "Am I choosing the right strategy?" "Which is the best stage of the market cycle to invest?" "Should I focus on timing the market, or should I pay more attention to time *in* the market?"

After working with thousands of investors who go through the same cycle and have similarities when it comes to what's holding them back and helping them get out of it, we developed a framework that can be used whether you're just getting started or are about to pivot and scale your portfolio. We've applied this framework at various times in our own business, and it has always yielded results.

FACTORS THAT HOLD NEW INVESTORS BACK

The reluctance of many aspiring real estate investors to launch a real estate venture is multifaceted and can be attributed to a variety of factors.

LACK OF KNOWLEDGE OR EXPERIENCE WITHIN THE REAL ESTATE INDUSTRY

An aspiring real estate investor may not have a thorough understanding of the industry and the various nuances that come with it. When we first got started, we had to learn the basics by trial and error, such as figuring out how to analyze deals, how to determine property values, property laws, market trends, and negotiation strategies. This learning curve can make it difficult for new investors to make informed decisions and increase their chances of success.

Additionally, nine-to-fivers who are inexperienced in owning their own business have a hard time understanding the intangible elements of being a real estate investing business owner. As a real estate investor, you are often working independently and may not have the support and camaraderie of a traditional work environment—there's no walking up to a water cooler to have a quick chat about something you're struggling with. Also, you are often dealing with a variety of vendors, such as contractors, real estate agents, and property managers, who may not always have the same goals or priorities as you. This can lead to conflicts and difficulties in coordination and communication. In contrast, in a traditional job setting, you typically have a clear hierarchy and defined roles and responsibilities, which can make it easier to work with your coworkers and manage any conflicts that may arise.

UNCERTAINTY AND LACK OF CONFIDENCE IN ABILITY TO SUCCEED

Many investors who lack a clear understanding of the real estate industry may feel unsure of their ability to succeed. This can lead to a lack of confidence in their own abilities, making it even more difficult to take action and move forward with their investment plans.

A significant change from a traditional W-2 job to a running a real estate investing business is that there is no set vision that you are handed by management. As a business owner, you need to craft your own vision and come up with a plan to achieve it.

It's often said that in business, the only limit to success is one's own imagination and drive. However, for many aspiring investors, the lack of set parameters can make it challenging to come up with a clear vision, which can be frustrating.

LACK OF FINANCIAL RESOURCES OR COMPREHENSIVE INVESTMENT PLAN

There is a common misconception that to start real estate investing, you need to already be wealthy. Without financial resources, investors may be unable to get started. Additionally, a comprehensive investment plan can help investors navigate the real estate industry and increase their chances of success. Without one, they may struggle to achieve their investment goals. However, these plans are very individual-specific, and there is no one-size-fits-all solution.

FEAR OF FAILURE

Fear of failure is a natural human emotion and can be a significant deterrent for many aspiring real estate investors. This fear can prevent them from taking action and pursuing their investment plans. It can impact even the brightest minds if not careful. In fact, we have found that the most educated nine-to-fivers (including ourselves) are the ones most affected by this fear.

The traditional education system can promote fear of failure by placing a heavy emphasis on grades and test scores as the primary measure of success, rather than on learning and personal growth. This can create a culture where students are more focused on avoiding failure than on taking risks and trying new things. Additionally, the traditional education system can create a competitive environment where students feel pressure to constantly outperform their peers, which can lead to feelings of inadequacy and fear of failure.

The corporate work environment can exacerbate the fear of failure promoted by the traditional education system by placing a similar emphasis on performance and success. In a corporate setting, employees are often evaluated based on their productivity and the results they produce, rather than on their effort and learning. This can create a culture where employees are afraid to take risks or try new things for fear of being seen as incompetent or failing to meet expectations. Additionally, the corporate work environment can foster a competitive culture where employees are constantly vying for promotions, raises, and recognition, which can increase the pressure to succeed and make the fear of failure worse.

LACK OF ACCESS TO NECESSARY SUPPORT AND RESOURCES

Starting a real estate investment venture can be a complex and challenging process. Aspiring investors may benefit from mentorship and guidance from experienced professionals, as well as access to funding. Without these resources, it can be difficult to navigate the industry and achieve investment goals.

Large organizations often have formal training and development programs for employees, as well as established mentorship and coaching programs. These programs are designed to help employees acquire the skills and knowledge they need to advance in their careers and meet the needs of the organization. In contrast, the real estate industry is a more decentralized and fragmented market where individual investors and small companies may not have the same resources, programs, and support as larger corporations. Additionally, real estate investors may not have the same access to capital, expertise, and networking opportunities as employees in a corporation do.

Overall, the corporate environment may provide more structured access to resources and mentorship for employees than the real estate market does for investors.

LACK OF ROLE MODELS

We faced another problem that you may relate to. When we were starting out in our investing journey, most real estate investors we saw were spending forty to sixty hours a week growing their real estate portfolio. Their method of running the business did not resonate with us because we didn't want to be at the job site every day and we didn't want to answer tenant phone calls. The lack of role models to look up to and business models we could replicate were some of the toughest challenges we had to navigate as brand-new real estate investors.

Role models can be an important source of inspiration and guidance, provide examples of what is possible, and serve as a source of motivation to overcome obstacles and achieve success.

As the famous entrepreneur and motivational speaker, Tony Robbins, said: "A role model is someone who is living proof that your dream is possible."

Having someone to look up to and emulate would help a new real estate investor stay focused on their goals and learn from the successes and failures of others. Role models can also provide valuable insights and advice on how to navigate the business world and make smart decisions. They can serve as a sounding board for ideas and provide feedback and guidance on how to improve. Additionally, having a role model can also help develop a sense of belongingness and community, which can be beneficial to personal and professional growth.

The lack of role models for corporate professionals trying to scale their real estate portfolio moonlighting as real estate investors makes it is difficult to visualize the end result.

ANALYSIS PARALYSIS

Analysis paralysis, a phenomenon that can occur when an individual is presented with an overwhelming number of options or is uncertain about the potential consequences of their choices. It's a natural reaction of the brain when it is confronted with a vast array of options, and it can lead to indecision.

However, it is important to understand that this phenomenon can be overcome by developing a more holistic approach toward decision-making. As the late Steve Jobs once said, "You can't connect the dots looking forward; you can only connect them looking backward. So, you have to trust that the dots will somehow connect in your future." Trusting in one's intuition and gaining a deeper understanding of oneself and one's values is key to making decisions that align with our true selves, rather than getting caught up in the fear of potential negative outcomes.

Remember that decision-making is not only about choosing the right option, it's also about the process of self-discovery and growth. A holistic approach to decision-making empowers us to make choices that align with our values and lead to a more fulfilling and authentic life. As Confucius said, "It does not matter how slowly you go as long as you do not stop." This approach allows us to navigate the complexity of decision-making with a clearer and more centered perspective.

Let's take a look at Raza's story to gain some perspective on this concept.

When Raza started investing, he was in a similar position as many other investors. He lacked commitment to a single investment strategy. However, he did try his hand at real estate.

For a while, he tried flipping properties. He also experimented with rentals. And then he decided to change course again. He attended many real estate meetups and conferences and each time, he was inspired by a new idea and strategy. However, what was seemingly a great way to sharpen his skills is what was actually holding him back.

We meet many investors who have been going to conferences and meetups for years. They are pretty much walking encyclopedias on all things real estate. If knowledge and dabbling alone could get us to early retirement, they'd be on the right track, but as it turns out, they are not even close to it.

Raza committed to the BRRRR strategy and his property avatar. This eliminated a great deal of the confusion and analysis paralysis. Within his first couple of months, Raza bought a distressed property for $60,000.

He put in about $15,000 for renovation. He had about $7,000 in soft costs. Once the property was rented out and cash flowing, he refinanced it. The appraisal showed that the value came to a whopping $110,000. He created approximately $28,000 in equity on that single deal. After refinancing, he not only pulled all of his money out, but he was also able to keep the property and collect passive cash flow each month. Then we decided to uplevel his game. His portfolio is over $2 million, and he did it in just a few years. His latest BRRRR deal made him over $200,000 in equity—and we are talking about a single deal.

Here is a step-by-step process to stop hesitating and move forward with your first deal. Follow these steps, and you'll be on your way toward building a solid real estate portfolio. We have designed an acronym to help you remember and implement them: "A-B-L-E." This is the action framework Raza used to get success.

THE ABLE FRAMEWORK

ABLE is a framework we developed for ourselves years ago when we first started as real estate investors. Each time we upleveled our game, we lost a lot of time in analysis paralysis. We had to develop a framework so we could take action faster each time. Growth is the game you play as a real estate investor and business owner—the better you get at growth, the faster you achieve success.

A – AVATAR

There are many ways to invest in real estate, and in hearing success stories of those that are where new investors need to be, most investors forget to focus on the key element to success: how these success stories got started. most investors with multi-million-dollar portfolios didn't start that way unless they were trust fund babies. We didn't come from money and neither do most of the folks we work with privately. for most of us, getting started in a way that allows us to take lower risks first is the right path.

Focus on these threess to define your initial low risk property avatar:

Small: Start with something small, for example, a three-bed/one-bath single-family row home in the city or a small ranch in the suburbs. A smaller investment is a great playground for a new investor. It allows you to learn from your mistakes while limiting your risk. Figuring out how to find a BRRRR-able property is like riding a bike, and it's much easier to learn how to ride a balance bike before riding it.

One example of a real estate investor who started small and scaled up is Robert Kiyosaki, the author of *Rich Dad, Poor Dad*. He started by investing in small rental properties and eventually built a real estate portfolio worth millions of dollars.

Another great example is Barbara Corcoran. She began her career with a $1,000 loan and eventually built one of the most successful real estate companies in New York City. She has been quoted saying, "I learned the hard way that it doesn't matter how many times you fail, you only have to be right once."

Taking smaller risks first can be beneficial because it allows you to gain experience and build confidence in your ability to manage risk. It can also help you identify and address potential issues before they become bigger problems. Additionally, if a small risk does not go as planned, the potential consequences will likely be less severe.

There is data that supports the idea of gradually increasing risk-taking over time. For example, research in the field of behavioral finance has shown that people who invest small amounts of money in the stock market on a regular basis tend to be more successful in the long-term than those who make infrequent, large investments. This is known as dollar-cost averaging, and it can help to mitigate the impact of market volatility on an investment portfolio.

Another study by John Coates, a neuroscientist, who studied traders in the City of London, found that the traders who took smaller risks in the beginning of their career and gradually increased their risk taking as they gained experience were more successful and lasted longer in the job than those who took larger risks early on.

In summary, taking smaller risks initially can be beneficial because it allows you to gain experience and build confidence in your ability to manage risk, and studies have shown that gradually increasing risk-taking over time can lead to better long-term outcomes.

Simple: Find something simple. It may not be the best deal of your life, but it will help you get started with a lower-risk investment. Raza made $28,000 in equity on his first BRRRR deal, and his latest deal made him close to ten times that amount. That is the power of starting simple and scaling it further. Remember, this is your first deal, not your only deal. If you have no construction experience, we recommend going with a cosmetic rehab. We know you're thinking, "Yes, but shells are better deals." We agree; however, they're also going to be a steep learning curve on working with contractors, permits, etc. To learn how to BRRRR, start with a simpler project and then move your way up to a more complicated one.

Scalable: We get emails every day from new investors who are just starting out. They want to know how to negotiate a FSBO ("for sale by owner"), how they can do a "subject-to" deal, how to buy a property with a cloudy title, and the like. On the other hand, the property avatar would be something you can pick up again and again, instead of something you have to figure out every single time. This is the way to build a large portfolio without losing your mind and learning something from scratch on every single deal.

In any business, the ability to consistently produce the same results over time is important for a number of reasons, including quality control, cost management, and customer satisfaction. In the context of real estate investing, this would mean producing great rental rehabs, keeping the renovation costs down, and providing a safe environment repeatably to your tenants.

One key aspect of repeatability is having well-defined processes in place. This includes clear instructions for how tasks should be performed, as well as guidelines for how to handle variations and exceptions. By having these processes in place, real estate can ensure that your team members are working in a consistent and efficient manner, which can help to improve quality and reduce costs. The variations and exceptions can be discovered and the processes around them can be put in place over time.

Repeatability also allows effective monitoring and measurement. This includes tracking key performance indicators (KPIs) such as construction budget and schedule, soft costs, time on the market when trying to find a tenant, and maintenance costs. By monitoring these KPIs, real estate investors with a repeatable and scalable avatar can identify areas where improvements are needed and make adjustments accordingly, which can help to improve repeatability over time.

Overall, repeatability is a critical aspect of any business especially real estate investing and plays an important role in maintaining and improving quality, reducing costs, and satisfying customers (a.k.a. tenants). This also allows real estate investors to ensure that they are able to consistently produce the same results over time.

B – BLINDERS

Brain imaging studies have shown that the reward centers of the brain are activated when people are presented with new and uncertain opportunities, which may help explain why entrepreneurs are often drawn to "shiny objects." "The neuroeconomics of entrepreneurship" by Scott Shane, published in the Journal of Management in 2014, reviews research on the neural mechanisms underlying entrepreneurial decision-making and highlights the role of the ventral striatum and the ventromedial prefrontal cortex in processing rewards and evaluating opportunities.

Entrepreneurs may get excited by "shiny objects" because they are constantly on the lookout for new and innovative ideas or technologies that can give them a competitive advantage in their industry. This is known as "opportunity seeking" and is a common trait among successful entrepreneurs.

If you have an entrepreneurial mindset—and we're assuming you do since you're investing in real estate as opposed to the cookie cutter path most people take—putting your blinders on may sound scary. With so much information available, it can be tempting to pursue every opportunity that comes your way.

However, successful entrepreneurs understand the importance of ignoring the temptation to chase after "shiny objects" because it can distract from their core business and lead to wasted resources and lost opportunities. Instead, they should concentrate on building a strong and sustainable business by identifying and capitalizing their unique strengths and resources. Chasing after "shiny objects" and pursuing too many opportunities may lead to a lack of focus and direction, making it difficult for entrepreneurs to achieve their goals.

Jeff Bezos, the founder and former CEO of Amazon, is an example of a successful entrepreneur who avoided the urge to chase after "shiny objects." Bezos focused on building a strong and sustainable business by identifying and leveraging his company's unique strengths in online retail. Rather than diversifying into other areas, he concentrated on expanding and improving Amazon's core business. This focus helped Amazon to become one of the most successful and valuable companies in the world.

Bezos's approach to business was to focus on the long-term and avoid distractions, as he said, "I very frequently get the question: 'What's going to change in the next ten years?' And that is a very interesting question; it's a very common one. I almost never get the question: 'What's not going to change in the next ten years?' And I submit to you that that second question is actually the more important of the two—because you can build a business strategy around the things that are stable in time."

Let's now apply this concept to real estate investing. Many real estate investors dabble in various areas, but those who pursue too many opportunities rarely scale their rental portfolio quickly.

Now when you look at real estate investors who are using creative ways to build their empires, it is easy to focus on the end results, the lifestyle, and maybe even the journey. Almost no one pays attention to those initial steps. Therefore, in this chapter, we will focus on the part that is most important for almost all new investors—getting started.

Most, if not all, new investors that are successful at scaling start simply. They take some time to define what they want and what they're comfortable with before going after it. But they do it with their blinders on—they stick to the plan. They stay away from shiny things, and they move forward with their strategy and avatar in mind.

Sure, there may come a time when you spot a better deal. Perhaps someone comes along and presents you with an offering you simply have to consider. Then, when you check it out, you find that investors are fighting to get it. It has great potential.

However, maybe you're not entering a fair fight. Perhaps you don't have the capital or borrowing capacity to turn it into your most profitable deal. Maybe it's outside your targeted area and has nothing to do with your regular tenant pool.

You'd risk jumping blindly into the deal, perhaps taking on more than you could handle.

We're not saying that you won't get to that stage eventually. Yet, in the early stages, it's not something worth thinking about. It's better to stick with what you know and what you're comfortable with. There's lower risk involved, mistakes aren't as costly, and you can repeat the process until you master it. You can actively scale the strategy and build your empire. So, once you have your avatar, put your blinders on to keep distractions at bay.

L – LEAP OF FAITH

Your leap of faith starts with the "why." Your "why" carries significant weight.

A person's "why" refers to the underlying reason or purpose for their actions or decisions. In the context of real estate investing, a person's "why" is the reason why they have chosen to invest in real estate and what they hope to achieve through that investment. This could be to generate a steady stream of passive income, build wealth over time, achieve financial independence, or any other personal financial goal.

As we discussed, our "why" was the desire to have control over our time. We didn't need a bigger motivation than time to take action. No analysis, spreadsheet, or convincing from others could give us a greater drive.

Not even the potential shame of failing was bigger than this "why."

Everyone's reasons for achieving financial goals may differ, but for a working parent looking to make a transition and take control of their life, this is likely the driving force behind every decision. Once you have your "why," your conviction will have the right foundation.

Here are a few ways that a person's "why" can help them take the leap of faith:

MOTIVATION

Having a clear understanding of why they want to invest in real estate can help a person stay motivated and committed, even when faced with uncertainty or obstacles.

As we reflect on the time when we had our two children back-to-back, that was the period of our lives when we felt the most motivated. Even after late nights of nursing, we still had the energy to look at properties while grabbing a quick cup of coffee in the morning before the newborn and the toddler woke up. We were so motivated that no amount of fatigue that every new parent faces made us want to stop. At times, it felt like we were operating at superhuman capacity, which was something we had never seen in ourselves before. We worked with a sense of fervor we had never felt before, with an almost uncontrollable urge to figure out how to achieve our goals.

Find the "why" that allows you to work with that kind of fervor. This is going to be your catalyst to put things in motion.

CONFIDENCE

Knowing their "why" can give a person the confidence they need to make a decision and take action. It can help them to believe in themselves and their ability to achieve their goals.

As we look back when we first got started, we laugh at ourselves and our naïve confidence. The offers we put in, the brazen negotiating we applied, the recklessness with which we able to pick up the phone and call complete strangers to discuss lending, new deals, or simply to make a connection was not something we was used to seeing ourselves implement. We were not in tune with the nuances of etiquette with which business owners connected with each other. Looking back, we are grateful for those people who did not put us down despite our shameless confidence. In hindsight, we also understand what worked in our favor. Our "why" was always so clear and authentic, we had no reason to hide behind our lack of experience. Such truthful confidence can be magnetic and can allow the people you come in contact with to let their guard down and enjoy the refreshing outlook you exhibit.

CLARITY

Knowing one's "why" can help individuals gain a clear understanding of their goals and desired achievements. This clarity can assist in making more informed decisions while avoiding distractions that don't align with their goals.

The clearer we got with what kind of lifestyle we were after, the easier the decision making and taking action got. We were certain that we didn't want to revolve life around business; we wanted it to be the other way around. We were going to build a business around the life we wanted. This clarity was simple to understand but difficult to implement, and it allowed us to eliminate 90 percent of the options in front of us. Decision making became easier because of the extreme clarity we operated with. We had no idea we were operating differently than everyone else. We were so deeply committed and devoted to our "why" that we never realized we was thinking out of the box. It wasn't until other investors started asking questions about our strategy and tactics that we realized how far we had come, and we can attribute this to extreme clarity. Things were so clear to us, we had never even given any other option any thought.

ALIGNMENT

Knowing one's "why" can also help a person to align with like-minded individuals or groups who share similar goals and values, which can provide support, guidance, and mentorship. This communication strengthens the "why" and helps crystallize it further. Cementing this "why" allows new real estate investors to get closer to taking the leap of faith when it is time. The more you talk about your story and your "why", the stronger your alignment will become.

In summary, having a clear understanding of one's "why" can provide the motivation, confidence, clarity, and alignment needed to take the leap of faith when it comes to real estate investing. Taking a leap of faith begins with the conviction that your life cannot continue the way it is currently. With faith, you can make a change and find success.

Developing the conviction for change can be challenging, but there are several helpful ways to build the conviction needed to make a change. Here are a few ways to develop the conviction for change:

Understand the benefits. Research the benefits of making a change and understand how it will positively impact your life. Understanding the potential positive outcomes can help you to develop the conviction to make a change. In reality, once you make a decision, it isn't that hard to find enough benefits to help you take action. The decision in front of us is usually not as important as we think. Many factors in our journey forward can make or break our trajectory, not just the current decision.

Identify the costs of not taking the leap of faith. Consider the costs of not making a change, including the potential negative impacts on your life. This can help you to understand the importance of making a change and develop the conviction to do so.

Sure, there is opportunity cost that can be calculated numerically. However, there is the cost of missing out on an impending tipping point for personal growth. These tipping points can be valuable in our growth trajectory. And missing out on these can shrink the momentum that was built in trying to get to that level.

Get support. Surround yourself with people who support your decision to make a change. We had an unspoken agreement to support each other in making tough decisions and then following through with the support when the decision turned out to be wrong. Most decisions lead to either success or learning opportunities, and once you find someone—whether it is a spouse, a parent, a friend, a business partner, or an accountability group—your general sense of well-being as a real estate investor will improve considerably. If possible, seek out the guidance and advice of those who have successfully made similar changes.

Unfortunately, most of us do not have a support system built into our lives. Instead, you will have to seek it out and build a community. This is the community you call upon when you are on the verge of taking the leap of faith. These are friends who will understand you when you have something to share that most people around wouldn't understand.

Take small steps. Start with small, manageable steps toward making a change, and build momentum as you gain confidence in your ability to make the change.

Incremental growth is one of the most undervalued elements of scaling a business and personal development. Small incremental growth steps are not only important in terms of achieving tangible goals, but they also play a crucial role in personal and professional development, providing an opportunity to reflect on one's progress and make adjustments as necessary. These small steps can lead to significant transformations over time and help us to become more resilient, adaptive, and open to new opportunities. They also help us to develop a growth mindset, allowing us to see challenges as opportunities for learning and development rather than obstacles. In short, small incremental growth steps can be seen as the building blocks of progress and success, both in business and in life.

Reflect on your values. Reflect on your values and how making a change aligns with them.

When a change aligns with one's values, it is not only easier to build the conviction to make it happen, but it also has a deeper meaning and purpose. When we make changes that align with our values, we are more likely to feel fulfilled and satisfied with the direction of our lives. We are more likely to stay committed to the change and to see it through to completion. In business, when a change aligns with the values of business we are set to build, it is more likely to be embraced by vendors and team members, leading to a more united and motivated team that feels like a community, and at times, a movement. Reflecting and implementing value-based changes are more likely to lead to long-term success and a positive impact on society.

Furthermore, when a change aligns with one's values, it goes beyond a mere action or decision—it becomes an expression of who we are and what we stand for. It represents a deeper sense of self-awareness and authenticity, leading to a more authentic and fulfilling life and real estate investing business. It is a powerful reminder that success is not only about achieving external goals but also about staying true to oneself and living in alignment with one's values.

In summary, when a change aligns with one's values, it not only makes it easier to build the conviction to make it happen but also it has a profound impact on one's personal and professional development, leading to a more meaningful and fulfilling life and business.

Be mindful of your thoughts and beliefs. Be mindful of the thoughts and beliefs that may be holding you back from making a change and work on shifting them to a more positive perspective.

Ultimately, developing the conviction for change takes time, effort, and a willingness to step out of your comfort zone. With persistence and determination, you can build the conviction you need to make a change and take the leap of faith. Ask yourself: What could go right?

LEARN HOW TO QUANTIFY AND MITIGATE RISKS

Quantitative risk management is the process of converting the impact of risk on a project into numerical terms. This numerical information is often used to determine the cost and time contingencies of the project. For instance, if you're analyzing your first BRRRR deal and you suspect your numbers are around $10,000 off. If your worst-case scenario becomes a reality, consider that $10,000 an investment in your education, and it's unlikely that you'll make that same mistake again.

We overpaid on our first investment property by $15,000, which was a significant hit on our family's reserves at the time. Nevertheless, we still managed to build a multi-million-dollar, cash-flowing real estate portfolio. And guess what? We never made the same mistake again. At one point, we had a theft incident at one of our properties, but we handled it with poise, and our contractor was surprised how well we took it. No fingers were pointed, and no sleep was lost; we simply treated it as part of the business and incorporated it into our contingency plan. Lesson learned: we will change the locks on any property we acquire the very same day we close the deal on it.

One way to mitigate risks is by developing resilience and a growth mindset. Resilience is the ability to bounce back from adversity, and a growth mindset is the belief that one's abilities can be developed through effort. These two qualities help to build a sense of confidence and self-reliance, allowing us to approach challenges with a sense of optimism and determination.

Moreover, by being aware of our values and priorities and making choices and take actions that align with them, we can avoid taking unnecessary risks and instead focus on opportunities that align with our goals.

E – EXPECTATIONS

If there's one thing we'd like to change about the real estate investing industry, it's the unrealistic perspectives that many investors have. The "fake it till you make it" mentality may inspire some, but we believe it can also hurt other investors just as much as it inspires. That's why we strive to give you a realistic perspective on the process of real estate investing. Like any business venture, it has its ups and downs. Sometimes we step on ladders, and sometimes we step on snakes.

One of the biggest goals for any real estate investor is taking control of their life; wealth and freedom contribute toward that control. However, it's a long journey to reach that peak.

Until you reach the summit, it's important to remember that not everything is under your control every step of the way. Taking a leap of faith is a crucial step that can bring you relief, confidence, and even make you proud that you put out that first offer on a property.

After you take the leap, it's important to manage your expectations. Remember that your first offer is the hardest decision, and dipping your toes in the water does not come easy. However, at the same time, manage your expectations and don't expect your first time to be a Cinderella story. That one offer might not be your magic bullet to retirement; it might take a few tries.

Some neighborhoods or market cycles can be highly competitive, and sellers are showered with offers from tons of investors. It could take you a few tries to get the first offer under contract. Nothing is given, everything is earned, and not everyone is operating on a level playing field.

Even the property investment game is a stream of wins and losses. You can be ten years into building and growing your real estate empire and still not get every deal that you want.

We hope that the ABLE framework provides you with a series of steps you can follow to feel more comfortable with your first deal. It's also a self-realization process that will prevent you from quitting if things don't go your way quickly enough.

Most importantly, it's a method of snapping out of analysis paralysis and taking your first steps toward getting the first property under contract. It could happen tomorrow, a week, or two months from the moment you decide to transition into becoming a real estate investor, but the more you try, the easier everything becomes.

The only way you won't succeed is with inaction.

PROGRESS OVER PERFECTION

Time is the most valuable resource you have in your professional and personal life—not money. As employees or business owners who are trading hours for dollars, we are coerced into undervaluing our time. Even when we understand, in theory, that our time is more valuable than money, it becomes tough to apply it in practice when making business decisions.

This requires a major mindset shift. How you manage your time will determine how you select deals or whether you take action.

It is easy to convince yourself that you can trade time for perfection. Many investors fall into this trap, believing that the more they search, the more they pace themselves, the more they will achieve. However, the belief that the perfect life-changing decision is out there, just waiting to be found, is an intelligent person's way of keeping themselves in their comfort zone.

In reality, the very concept of perfection is the enemy. Real estate investing and perfection do not mix. Perfection can grow to be the biggest obstacle in your path. It may even be an immovable obstacle if you waste too much of your most precious resource—time.

Action over perfection is always the shortest route toward your goals. It teaches you to start small and gradually grow. It will give you experience, confidence, expose you to new opportunities, and accelerate your wealth. Before long, you might find yourself in a place that feels perfect because it's already beyond what you originally envisioned. And you may start re-defining what perfection means to you.

MEET ROCKSTAR INVESTOR PUJA

Puja was a pharmacist by trade, but she always aspired to get involved in real estate. Once Puja could identify what she needed to work on, with support from a community, she discovered accountability—a powerful tool that she used to actually implement strategy and go after her goals.

Taking the first step became easy when she implemented this framework and figured out how to empower herself to take action.

And that's something you can accomplish with the ABLE framework too.

CHAPTER ELEVEN
Balancing Social Impact and Profitability

Some people have an aversion to making money. However, we don't view money as evil or investors as solely focused on personal profit. Naturally, when you're building your business or portfolio, you have to make money; however, that doesn't mean you can't have a positive impact. You can balance social impact with profitability. If you really care about the community, you should look at real estate investments as a platform. It can create opportunities to get more involved, bring like-minded investors together, fix problems, and so on. And if you keep in mind the four elements we'll discuss in this chapter, it'll be even easier.

ELEMENT NO. 1: HELPING TO REMOVE BLIGHT

If you're new to real estate, it's important to understand the term "blight." By definition, a property affected by blight is a space no longer considered in a beneficial condition to its community.

Blighted properties have lost their value as economic commodities and may not even be considered functional living spaces. In essence, blight refers to a specific stage in which a real estate asset can find itself—depreciation. Blight is something you'll see in every type of community, whether urban, rural, and suburban areas.

So, how does blight happen?

It really depends on the area, but common causes include the lack of investment and industry withdrawals that are followed by massive unemployment. Unemployment leads to worker migration, which causes increased vacancy rates, abandonment, and property deterioration. When vacancies increase, local tax revenue often decreases, and local authorities typically respond by minimizing public services. In many cases, they even reduce the amount of code enforcement.

This creates a somewhat vicious circle as areas with low code enforcement aren't as attractive to buyers. It makes it hard for buyers to get good mortgages in neighborhoods containing blighted properties. Everything is undervalued, and so the population numbers in blighted areas continue to drop.

Of course, this isn't exactly a surprise to seasoned investors. These appraisal gaps often happen when market prices are much higher than appraised values. A lack of sales in the area can be the primary culprit.

Now, this does make things interesting for a specific type of buyer: the investor. Homeowners might not be attracted to blighted communities. However, the appraisal gap cap creates ideal conditions for investors instead of owner-occupiers.

According to recent studies from the Center for Community Progress (CCP), blight can cost hundreds of millions of dollars in property value losses. It costs local governments millions in tax revenue and can also rake up millions in repair budgets. Vacant and unattended properties can become safety hazards, and they can also contribute to spikes in crime rates.

As you can see, blight is responsible for a wide range of social and environmental health problems. Interestingly enough, most experts would agree that blight isn't an inherited problem. In fact, it's a more complex issue created by modern market forces, socio-economic changes, and public policies.

So, where do you fit in as an investor?

Although many of the existing policies continue creating blighted areas, there are plenty of anti-blight policies as well. Local governments implement these piecemeal approaches in the hope of increasing the economic wealth of affected places.

This is good news because many anti-blight programs are targeted toward the private sector, engaging private investors to get involved with revitalizing distressed neighborhoods. Many such programs have greening projects in place to beautify the land and make it market-ready for when developers return. In other cases, local governments will rely on community-driven organizations to get involved and breathe new life in blighted neighborhoods.

As an investor, you have a couple of opportunities when researching areas known for their blighted properties.

First, with the right programs in place, you can buy an asset at a bargain. Once the community gets back on its feet, your return on investment can be substantial. Second, you can modernize old structures and restore their functionality. The fewer blighted properties in an area, the smaller the appraisal gap. Furthermore, no one likes living in a blighted area—that goes for both owner-occupiers and tenants.

You can bring money into a community in many ways. You could buy blighted properties for the land underneath and develop modern housing units over the old structure, but you could also buy functional properties. Spending money in that market means that some of the cash goes to the local government, and these funds that can be reinvested in the community to deal with blighted properties, restore the aesthetics, and improve the living conditions for everyone.

If you make more deals in an area, repeating this would help eliminate much of the blight, instantly improving the living conditions. As your portfolio, capital, and influence grow, you could take on more ambitious projects to combat blight.

ELEMENT NO. 2: SOLVING THE AFFORDABLE HOUSING SHORTAGE

Most people are familiar with the Great Recession, the Great Financial Crisis, and the Dot-Com bubble burst. However, fewer realize the American economy has been hit by something else in recent years—the Great Affordability Crisis.

A discrepancy existed between how people spent their money and what they earned. The 2010s looked great on paper, with low unemployment rates and high incomes, but many researchers agree that landlords, hospital administrators, and even childcare centers bled families dry. This affected millions of Americans, and you might not have noticed without looking at it from a cost-of-living prism.

Around two in five American adults found it difficult to put together $400 in case of an emergency. These days, one in five adults struggles to pay their monthly bills. While the country kept generating wealth, one in three American households is considered by all standards—financially fragile. Rising inequality, slower productivity growth combined with the spiraling cost of living best describe the current American economic life.

Policy solutions are promised from local to federal levels, but they never seem to materialize. This further slows down productivity and growth and keeps many families from achieving their dreams of security.

One of the most damaging elements is the price of housing. Low and middle-income families have little to no chance of buying a home in a central location in an urban area where jobs are available. New York and the Bay Area are the most extreme examples of the housing crisis.

That said, it's more of a national problem, constantly fueled by restrictive building codes, underinvestment, and stagnant wages.

In up to 80 percent of metro regions, prices are outpacing wage increases. Even rural areas are now taking a big hit post-recession due to sluggish income growth. Many households in North Carolina and Texas are reportedly paying over half their income on housing expenses. As a result, homeownership has fallen considerably. For example, Millennials have an ownership rate eight points lower than their parents, back when they were at the same age. The U.S. has around 3.5 million young families that are forced to rent. This caused a considerable delay in wealth accumulation for Millennials and Gen X representatives.

Additionally, rent isn't affordable. Many landlords have raised their prices faster than wages have increased for renters—a trend that's been happening for decades. Naturally, this can put pressure on you as an investor and would-be landlord. If people can't afford anything these days, how can you make money and help others in the process?

Well, this is where we want to talk to you about the Section 8 Voucher Program. Section 8 is a Housing Choice Voucher Program backed by funding from the U.S. Department of Housing and Urban Development, otherwise known as HUD. It's not a public housing program. Instead, it provides rent subsidies for Americans with low-income salaries.

Beneficiaries can use a voucher to apply for rental housing. This program is administered by local housing authorities. They review applications, screen recipients and landlords, inspect properties, and so on.

The advertised advantages include:

- Lower vacancy rates
- Potential to charge higher rent
- Reliable, timely payments

A significant number of landlords refuse to accept vouchers, exacerbating the housing affordability crisis. However, you can take a different approach. You can look at Section 8 as a core part of your investment strategy.

Besides, this is another way you can give back. You can do your part as a real estate investor by buying rental units and providing affordable housing to low-income individuals and families. By doing so, you can contribute to the solution instead of being part of the problem and raise the standards of living. And the government checks will guarantee you have the steady cash flow to continue growing.

ELEMENT NO. 3: RAISE THE BAR IN LOW-INCOME NEIGHBORHOODS

Section 8 housing has many predatory landlords. Most landlords know the financial situation of their tenants. They know about the Great Affordability Crisis, but they choose to be part of the problem. If you ask me, what's even worse is that predatory landlords flock to low-income neighborhoods; it's easier to take advantage of people who can't afford to go elsewhere. They assume that eventually, renters will make do with whatever they have to for a roof over their heads.

You won't see modern finishes and newly renovated apartments or houses. These landlords invest in properties that can generate passive income rather than investing in the tenant's comfort and safety. We would like to raise the bar on Section 8 housing.

HIGH-END FINISHES

Maybe you're considering skipping high-end finishes like granite countertops and stainless-steel appliances, believing they're not worth the investment. While they may not be essential, luxurious finishes create a wonderful experience for the tenants. Our environment has a direct impact on our self-worth and future vision, and providing a good space for our tenants allows us to create additional social impact.

As a business, we must also prioritize profitability alongside social impact. Happy tenants stay at your property longer, reducing your vacancy rates. Units with higher-end finishes also stay vacant for a shorter period of time during turnovers due to the better aesthetics compared to other rentals within a similar price range in the same neighborhoods. Keeping a low vacancy rate is instrumental to having a great long-term return on investment (ROI).

BETTER CUSTOMER SERVICE

Predatory landlords don't care about the well-being of their tenants. They demonstrate this not only through below average living conditions but also lackluster customer service.

Just a few months ago, we spoke to our contractor about a distressed property we were looking to acquire. He was beside himself after his walkthrough. This was a Section 8 property that was occupied. Our contractor went over how the tenant was in tears when he visited the property. She talked about how her landlord never answers the phone. Unless there is a Section 8 inspection due, the landlord is missing in action. These are practices that give landlords a bad rap. These landlords are the reason the term "slumlord" is used.

We recommend tracking the time it takes to answer a tenant requests. This is something we implemented early on in our business. Along with that, be sure to have written policies and expectations shared with the tenants so they understand how long they will have to wait for which type of maintenance request.

As investors, we have the opportunity to create social impact early in our journeys. Section 8 tenants are our customers. Treat this business like a hospitality business, and you will have created social impact without having to be born with a silver spoon.

MEET ROCKSTAR INVESTORS RENU AND JOHN

Renu and John are a lovely couple that had great jobs and lived in a beautiful penthouse apartment with the view of the New York skyline. However, they saw others ten years ahead of them burning out, and they aspired to leave it all behind for a life where they were financially free and also making social impact.

They were interested in investing and in the BRRRR strategy but the method of execution seemed out of reach. Their first out-of-state deal allowed them to create tens of thousands of dollars in forced appreciation within just a few months while being completely hands off, and cash flow for life on just that one deal. But the best part is, after their first BRRRR deal, they showed up more empowered than ever before because they were able to create social impact.

When we discuss social impact, we focus on how it is helpful to others. But we wanted to share this story because seeing this couple's lit up faces is evidence that social impact is also good for the person imparting it.

Evidence shows that helping others can also benefit our own mental health and wellbeing. It can reduce stress as well as improve mood and self-esteem, and it can leave us feeling happier. Feeling like part of something greater than oneself and seeing the power we have to touch lives can make us feel less alone in the universe and give us meaning. It can be empowering as an investor to know that you can create impact in others' lives even as you are starting out.

CHAPTER TWELVE

Adopting the Mindset of a Successful Investor

As you enter the penultimate chapter, we want to share another success story that aligns with our theme.

Before using the SCALE strategy, Michele struggled. She didn't have a high income and came into real estate right before the COVID-19 pandemic. Michele felt that she didn't know enough. She didn't trust her math and was lacking a lot in the confidence department. On her first BRRRR deal, Michele bought for $63,000 and she put $40,000 into renovations. She brought only a small fraction (10 percent of acquisition and zero percent of construction) to the table at closing. When she was done, the property appraised at $139,000, giving Michele a forced equity of $37,000—higher than her annual salary at the time. She made that in equity on her first deal as a rookie—a single deal.

Michele's background had nothing to do with real estate. She used to be a fitness professional. When Michele put her offer in, she was panicked. She had used funds from her HELOC to bring the seed money at the closing table. She not only paid the HELOC back, but she was also able to do multiple deals after that and make additional money each time.

Yet, with the right tools and mindset, she's well on her way to building her portfolio and securing her financial freedom. What impressed me even more was her starting with a low income just as COVID-19 started affecting the market.

If you want a success story like Michele's, this chapter is all about how you can get it. Let's talk about the final ingredient: adopting the mindset of a successful investor.

WHY MOST PEOPLE NEVER BUILD AND SCALE A REAL ESTATE PORTFOLIO

Even though so many people want to make work optional by investing in real estate, there are some common themes that stop investors from either getting started or scaling their real estate portfolio. We want to outline some of the general fundamentals of what holds most people back.

We speak to thousands of new investors with hunger to build wealth, passive income, and a life of freedom. After many conversations, we have developed an understanding of what most of us face as they get started. We can ourselves relate to many of these aspects since we ourselves had to face them when we got started. These issues could either prevent us from taking action or force us to take action and build wealth.

HIGH-EARNERS PARADOX

A high-income investor-to-be may have a cushy lifestyle. Unfortunately, high income provides enough money and comfort that can kill the motivation to invest in real estate.

We've already shared our personal experience with you at the start of this book. We had a great nine-to-five jobs with travel perks and an awesome career, but that all changed when we needed more flexibility and less stress. And while it's paradoxical, high income can stop you from building wealth if you're not careful.

CHOOSING PAINT COLORS INSTEAD OF PAINTING A FUTURE

As employees, we are often required to follow along with someone else's plan. The CEO of the company has a vision, and the employees are given goals and steps to align with that vision. This mentality can spill over into real estate investing. As the builder of an empire, you will need to first be the visionary, then develop goals, and then the tactics.

If your vision is your destination, your goals are your GPS. It's always better to try to figure out what kind of life you want before identifying the path and what steps to take. If you don't know where you want to get, how are you supposed to know how to get there? It's a new investor pitfall that can prevent you from getting started.

SHINY OBJECT SYNDROME

As we take new investors on their journey to financial independence, we often have conversations around "shiny objects." New investors may find a lot of ways to invest in real estate. We have found that committing to one single strategy that has stood the test of time is the single most way to scale fast.

Getting into real estate can allow you to explore everything, and trust me, it can feel exciting at first. But we aren't here to chase shiny objects. We are here to reach our higher potential and make work optional.

NO TIME

How many times have you said to yourself that you want to invest in real estate but you don't have the time? The truth is, most of us aren't really living lives set up to build wealth.

Society dictates our lives in a way that we can do our jobs, perform obligations, and maybe have some spare time. Actually, few people have their lives set up with that extra mental space to build wealth.

However, it's up to you to create time to carve space. It is important to understand that, generally speaking, with some exceptions, for nine-to-fivers the feeling of not having time is unrelated to a specific person and their specific circumstances. It's a privilege to follow the path of financial freedom and understand that life isn't made with magical time blocks for anyone with a traditional job. It's up to us as individuals to create the time.

There are CEOs that run billion-dollar companies and spend time with their families in the same twenty-four hours that we do. It is a matter of learning how to prioritize, outsourcing certain tasks, and possibly even eliminating time consuming activities that are less valuable.

We gave up binge-watching TV shows when we first got started, giving us hours back on a weekly basis that we could devote to real estate investing. Reflect on your own time-wasting activities, and ask yourself where you could carve out three to five hours per week.

NO ACCOUNTABILITY

Working for ourselves over the years, we've learned that we hold our commitments we make to others in higher regard than the commitment we make to ourselves. This is the reason we achieve better results when we work with others.

Real estate investing isn't the main topic of conversation at parties or when we get together with our loved ones. The lack of community and conversations surrounding this path can give us a feeling of being alone in this journey. Human beings are social animals, and having the support of like-minded individuals is key to success.

SUCCESS DOESN'T HAPPEN OVERNIGHT

Many of us have dedicated years to obtaining a degree in our respective fields and working our way up the corporate ladder. Despite years of being a nine-to-five employee, financial freedom still seems unattainable for many of us. When new investors enter the world of real estate, they often search for the magic bullet that will instantly grant them financial freedom, rather than earning it through hard work and dedication.

Real estate investing takes fraction of the time and effort compared to what we spend on our college education and our jobs to achieve financial freedom, but it does take some time. Stepping into the right investor mindset will help you seize lucrative opportunities faster and prevent you from wasting time and stagnating your wealth-building plans.

THE FOUR THINGS YOU CAN DO TO CREATE THE RIGHT MINDSET

Now it's time to give you a blueprint on how to create the proper mindset through four tried-and-true strategies.

1. Dare to Dream Big (and Escape the Hustle Mentality)

Most investors want more time with their families. Financial freedom is a way to earn that time back and gain newfound independence.

However, you're not going to reach that point if you don't allow yourself to dream big. You have to want to reach your fullest potential, and more importantly, you have to believe that your potential is greater than what you've been told.

There's still a right way and a wrong way to approach this. You see, for a while, I was hustling. It happened after I stabilized my business to go toward the path of financial independence. Believe it or not, this is not an uncommon trend among entrepreneurs. Hustling is the prevalent driving force behind many quick decisions. If you've ever hustled at anything, you probably felt the adrenaline rush. It's a captivating feeling. It motivates you and helps move things along, including in business.

While the hustler mentality is an acceptable starting point, you can't get stuck with it. It's a disruptive force in the long run. It can derail you from your path and even lead to burnout.

So, the first step to getting into the right mindset is to allow yourself to dream big. To do that, you have to escape the hustle mindset. Working hard to grab low-hanging fruit clutters your mind. If your mind is cluttered by tiny money-making opportunities, you won't be able to think clearly of bigger things, and you won't be able to focus on long-term growth.

Women specifically are often conditioned to be great at multi-tasking; therefore, we're often reluctant to outsource and tackle everything ourselves. Part of this has to do with social media influences and preconceptions in our society. If we're not succeeding simultaneously in every aspect of our lives, we're not doing a good job.

But venturing into entrepreneurship and real estate investing is a signal to declutter your to-do list. Start focusing on the big picture. Identify the things that bring you joy. Figure out what will burn you out and what will take you closer to your goal.

Make a habit out of doing a "time versus money" analysis. I'll never tell you to avoid working hard. I'm just proposing you work intentionally and don't waste your time. Leverage more of your time through outsourcing processes that don't require your direct input.

Successful investors always have scalability in mind, and this doesn't mesh with the hustle mindset. Hustling is more about making short-term decisions, while dreaming big is about profitable growth that will help you secure your future decades from now. Each learning curve or opportunity must be meaningful. You shouldn't spend time investing time and resources into projects that aren't scalable.

So, just how big can you dream?

Imagine setting a measurable five-year plan. For example, think about the number of rental units you'd like to own. When you dream big, multiply that goal by a factor of ten. As scary as it sounds, this ten-times rule of setting goals is used by successful investors and entrepreneurs in all industries.

Once you blow past your initial goal, you'll be able to look at your strategy and operations from a different perspective. You might discover that the way you've being going about business has been fine, but it may not be enough for a goal tenfold the initial one. Therefore, you'll start looking at what you can change to move in the right direction.

2. Ask Yourself What You Would Do if You Weren't Afraid

Our parents dreamed about seeing us in full-time jobs. They wanted us to have stability, and climbing the corporate ladder was our gold standard.

Once we landed managerial positions, our parents was thrilled. We'll admit, we were too, because we made them proud. But here's the problem with having a nine-to-five as your gold standard: It conditions you to be risk averse. The influx of steady paychecks makes you feel comfortable. Over time, you may not even notice the minimal yearly wage growth. Meanwhile, your mortgage payments, student debt, and everything else continue eating away at your earnings.

Then there's entrepreneurship.

Entrepreneurship comes with the blessed freedom of escaping the cycle, and as an investor, you're suddenly in charge of making your own rules. Most new business owners don't even see a glass ceiling. The limit is whatever they say it is, depending on the vision and drive. Even with plenty of prejudice thrown your way, you'll have more control. You'll learn to navigate those challenges.

Once you also enter a community of your peers, investing gets even more exciting. Integrity will earn you respect, and hard work (when focused in the right direction) pays off. Every good idea you have will ultimately benefit you and your business. This makes it seem like everyone should be an entrepreneur. Why would anyone great at something opt to work for someone else?

It's because entrepreneurship isn't always cheap. Liberty comes at a price. You have to set goals, make decisions, get out of your comfort zone, and more. Staying on a traditional career path means being in a low-risk cycle, where things come at ease.

Making this change doesn't come easy for everyone. Some, like myself, may even struggle with the very idea of being different. When everyone's sticking to the status quo, what makes you more different than becoming an entrepreneur?

However, this is the type of fear that you can overcome. Imagine what you could do without constraints? You could win the freedom that comes with being an entrepreneur and investor while also creating a low-risk passive income.

This is the kind of thinking that can help you pivot from the traditional gold standard. It's one way to think more like a successful investor and create the right mindset.

3. Speak Up (Loudly and Often)

Sometimes, I blamed my tactical engineering mindset for passing on various properties. On other occasions, I blamed my lack of experience at the time. We all get gut feelings and intuitions; our subconscious is trying to tell us things. I've had opportunities that felt amazing, but I didn't act on them. I wasn't able to justify my intuition with hard data.

Looking back, I'm not pleased with those decisions. It's not so much about passing on deals that would've turned out great. I wish I would've been more persistent and driven to figure out why my subconscious was pushing me to make a specific decision.

Intuition is by no means an asset when doing real estate math. Maybe gut feelings need to mature before you can trust them. But then I came to a different thought: how come we don't listen to ourselves more?

That's when it hit me.

We're not trained to be heard. As women, it's almost like a survival instinct passed down through generations.

Fortunately, we live in an environment that allows us to fight this instinct. We can start listening to ourselves and strive to achieve excellence. Working in corporate America or any male-dominated industry teaches women that boldness isn't a successful quality. I don't believe that to be true.

Our survival instinct is actually failing us. Let me ask you: how many times did you sell yourself short? How often did you believe you couldn't do something or sacrificed your emotional and physical well-being? Did you drop your dreams of financial independence because you believed a flawed woman is less of a challenge?

If you did, you're not alone.

Again, we weren't trained to think otherwise. But if there ever was a time to be more empowered, this is it. You have to start listening to yourself. Once you listen, you should speak up. This applies to all areas of your life, whether professional or personal.

And don't think about it as a motivational endeavor. Speaking up, and doing it loudly, is a critical skill set to master. It can make a big impact on your life and those around you. Confidence in your actions is key to making this change and getting closer to creating the right mindset.

4. Identify (and Escape) Your Busy Work

I decided to dive full-time into real estate a few months after giving birth to my second child. My first BRRRR property going under contract coincided with my son's birthday. By the time he turned three, my portfolio had a value of $4 million. It took me three years to cross the million-dollar revenue threshold, and that was right around the time I started my coaching business.

I had found my niche. I was good at presenting complex issues in easy-to-understand ways, and I could help others do it. Simultaneously, I experienced the freedom and fortune to start a new venture. But as amazing as the journey was for a while, my health began to decline. I couldn't separate the lines between business, health, kids, and myself. I wasn't motivated to make my health a priority. I was having more fun analyzing deals than exercising.

At that time, I was getting my own coaching. I knew the problem was with me, and a shift in my mindset would fix it. Still, knowing what I had to do didn't translate into action. I couldn't understand what was stopping me from doing what was necessary. Now that I look back, I think it came down to a matter of business growth becoming addictive.

I hired a holistic health coach and tried to become my best self-concerning health. It took only a month to get my first "Aha!" moment.

My biggest epiphany came when I was journaling. The simple act of writing by hand increases activity in the brain. This has a meditative and therapeutic effect which enhanced my mindfulness. Before long, I started having a more mindful approach in all areas of my life, including relationships, habits, sleep, parenting, business, etc. As a mindful entrepreneur, I realized that I had been wasting much of my time.

Back when my health was declining and I was gaining weight, I wasn't really working on the business. Many of my actions weren't intentional. I was going with the flow and got distracted by insignificant things. Now I have a new approach.

I try to stay away from activities that aren't aligned with strategy and purpose, rather, they're distractions that prevent you from reaching your long-term goals.

So, here's my last piece of advice:

Find your activities of meaning and significance. Let go of your busy work and figure out what moves the needle forward.

MEET ROCKSTAR INVESTOR OLIVIA

Olivia has been an active real estate investor since 2007, starting with wholesaling and then moving on to rehabilitation projects. Recently, she did rehab for the property she ended up calling her home.

But how did Olivia come to join the Open Spaces program? Well, Olivia knew me prior to signing up. Therefore, she was familiar both with my background and the people I surrounded myself with in the real estate space.

One of the things Olivia lacked was a methodical approach to building her portfolio. Her experience with wholesaling and flipping was different from mine. After being taught the SCALE strategy, Olivia gained some important knowledge. First, she learned about the value of leverage. This was a game-changer for her as Olivia came from a position where she would constantly raise capital to do any deals.

That methodology of hers often caused her to feel paralyzed while waiting to build the necessary capital. Now, Olivia is in a place where she has capital. She's able to leverage it, and she also understands the importance of that when it comes to scaling.

Although Olivia had some experience on the property market, she acknowledges that she had certain knowledge gaps. The new information, tips, and tools she received allowed her to improve her strategy moving forward.

Olivia understood that real estate isn't a get-rich-quick program. It's something you have to be committed to for the long haul. She appreciates the need to stay laser-focused on working toward her goals.

Through the SCALE strategy, Olivia was pushed in the right direction. She had a goal to get a property under contract by the end of the year. She managed to do that while in the thick of the program. But learning to take action wasn't the most valuable lesson for Olivia. To her, it was really a collection of lessons that saved her time and money. She invested in herself, her education, and she didn't have to learn many of the things she knows by making costly mistakes.

Olivia is a true success story. And sure, you can choose to focus on the fact that she didn't join the program with zero real estate experience. However, what she learned filled her knowledge gaps and changed her outlook on property investment—from how she finds deals, how she finances them, and the strategy she uses to build her equity and wealth.

CHAPTER THIRTEEN

Planning for the Future

Britta spent a lot of time researching real estate. However, she had yet to take any real action. Britta was stuck in a highly demanding job. She also had a beautiful family she loved spending time with, so she was apprehensive about taking on more.

How could she find the time?

When would she work on her portfolio?

Would she have to sacrifice her weekends or family time?

Where would she find the funds to buy and renovate properties?

How would she manage construction projects while having a full-time job?

Britta developed her strategy and started implementing it without distractions. By distilling her strategy and narrowing her scope, we eliminated 90 percent of the things she *thought* she should be doing and focused only on the 10 percent of the things she actually needed to do.

She learned how to get results, not by working hard and spending a lot of time researching, but by putting systems and processes in place to evaluate deals by looking at the numbers, getting funding for acquiring and renovating homes, and leveraging a great team so she wasn't spending all her time at the job site watching over her construction projects or doing property walkthroughs. She built a business that was scalable. Buying more properties would not mean a bigger time commitment.

Within just a few months, Britta acquired two properties and started renovating them. Her plan right now is to grow a multi-million-dollar portfolio in three years.

Building an impressive real estate portfolio isn't just about creating assets—it's about ensuring your time and location freedom.

MOST PEOPLE AREN'T PREPARED FOR RETIREMENT

A 2022 GO Banking Rates survey found that most Americans have less than $50,000 saved for retirement, citing that "36 percent have less than $10,000 saved and 27 percent have between $10,000 and $50,000."

But that's not the most disheartening discovery. The bigger problem is that most Americans consider their savings accounts or their retirement accounts as the primary method of retirement planning. As you are reading this, the money sitting in our savings accounts is literally losing value due to inflation. The money in your wallet today could be a fraction of its current value years from now.

Many of us don't realize that savings accounts have an appallingly low growth rate. The national return rate for most savings accounts is around 0.09 percent. That's a fraction of the annual inflation rate, which means that the money we put in our savings accounts can lose its value dramatically over time. Retirement accounts can have a higher return, but those will fluctuate too according to the term rate and how the market is doing. This nest egg, for many households, will no longer provide enough to cover basic living costs, travel, necessities, healthcare, and everything else during retirement. A 401(k) is vulnerable to the market's volatility as well.

Financial planners often come into picture for those that have savings and want to gain better returns. However, it is tough to give unbiased financial advice when your income depends on certain investments. It is important for us to get educated instead of relying on biased perception of financial planners.

The unfortunate reality is that most of us will end up working until our late sixties or early seventies due to poor retirement financial planning and lack of education. Your present financial situation might not be as gloomy as it seems once you work through your numbers. The reality is that plenty of Americans can afford to save if they shuffle their priorities. It's just a matter of sensing the need to do it and understanding how to manage their money.

Make no mistake—planning for the future is a must. And the earlier you start, the more time you have to build a robust portfolio that can ensure an early and comfortable retirement.

Throughout this book, we discussed the steps to financial, time and location freedom. In this final chapter, we want to walk you through the main takeaways that will set you up for success whether you are just starting your journey in real estate or you're looking to level up.

STRATEGIC PLANNING FOR FINANCIAL FREEDOM

Employees are forced to work hard on a plan for someone else's vision. But as the builder of your real estate empire, you will need to be the visionary first. You will need to create a strategic plan. Then use that plan to develop goals and then tactics.

If your vision is your destination, your goals are your GPS. It's always better to try to figure out what kind of life you want before identifying the path and what steps to take. If you don't know where you want to get, how are you supposed to know how to get there? It's a new investor pitfall that can prevent you from getting started.

We have outlined steps that you need to take to create your strategic plan. This will serve as your North Star as an investor.

Tip No. 1: Craft Your Vision for the Future
People spend more time and effort on planning a party than they do in creating a vision for their future. Take some alone time, and get rid of all distractions and craft your vision for a long-term future.

- How do you want to feel?
- Imagine your dream house. How does it feel like to live in your dream house?
- Imagine your dream car. How does it feel to drive your dream car?
- Imagine you have complete control over how you spend your time. Who are you spending your time with?
- Imagine you're in great shape physically. How does it feel to be in the best shape of your life?
- Let's talk about wealth. How does it feel to own more assets? How does it feel to be financially free?

Dream big! This is the time to really dream big, not incrementally better. If you think about it, we often want things that are incrementally better than what we have in the present. You can only do better from here, right?

You see, people tend to let society dictate the vision of their future. This can place limitations on what you believe you can achieve. Thus, it won't lead to the amazing outcomes you could otherwise have.

Imagine yourself starting with a blank slate. What would life look like from there?

It's important to use this approach for a number of reasons. Depending on what you want to achieve, you may need to stop doing some of the things you're doing in the present. Not every action or habit will take you where you want to go.

Taking a step back and crafting your vision can help you visualize the steps you need to take. And don't be afraid to go into detail. The clearer your vision, the greater the results you can achieve.

Think about the kind of legacy you want to leave behind. Imagine that you are eighty years old. Looking back, how would you want your life to have been? Going further into the future with your vision really helps put things into perspective, but you need to carve that time.

Consider the recent COVID-19 pandemic. Many people got the time to reflect on their lives and what they really wanted to do. People thought about their dreams and aspirations. They visualized their legacies and the things that made them happy.

When you're crafting your vision for the future, it doesn't have to be centered around monetary goals. Sure, that's a big part of what you're trying to achieve—financial security and freedom. However, it starts with being clear on where you want to go. Once you have that, you can start creating a financial plan with specific targets that will help you get there.

Tip No. 2: Figure Out Your "Why"

Finding out your "why" is a key part of planning your future. It's the process that enables you to discover what drives and motivates you to take action.

Whether you're starting a business, investing in real estate, growing a multi-million-dollar portfolio, you'll run into your share of hurdles. Failures and problems happen, even if you have a great strategy. Some things are unavoidable. But this is where your "why" or motivator comes in. A strong "why" will help you overcome challenges.

Many people don't have a strong drive to take action and plan their future. They're going about their daily lives with golden handcuffs on.

Not everyone is in a rough spot. Plenty of people have good jobs and good lives. They don't have much to complain about. What happens then? There's no need to plan for the future. People feel their lives are okay and don't want more. Perhaps they're even scared to dream of more as it would require breaking the routine—and our brains love routine.

This is where you can get stuck with the golden handcuffs. Once you become too comfortable and have a sense of security, anything new can seem risky.

For example, we thought we had it all figured out when we were in the corporate world. We believed that the higher up we went, the more control we'd gain over our time, and people would work for us and not the other way around. Needless to say, it didn't turn out like that. We soon realized that the higher up you go, the less time you have for your family.

This doesn't happen in entrepreneurship or investing because you control how you're going to run your business.

You shouldn't focus on everything you stand to lose from investing, saving, growing a business. Instead, you should focus of what you stand to gain. Think about that stuff to craft your vision. Follow your heart, passion, and goals. Don't subscribe to the negative part of the "what if" question.

As we shared in the previous chapter, a huge part of our why was time freedom, and we learned how real estate can afford us this. Once you get it right, it's a relatively passive form of investment. We're now growing our portfolio every year, but we don't spend more than an hour a day doing it! That leaves plenty of room to work on another business, travel, and spend time with family. Depending on your lifestyle goals, you can do whatever you want to do.

This is something you'll never be able to accomplish while working a regular nine-to-five job, regardless of how much money you're making.

Your vision and your "why" matter!

Our lifestyle goals to free up time put us on a unique journey in real estate. So, we adjusted our strategy to work toward our specific goals.

Tip No. 3: Reverse-Engineer to Create a Plan
Your vision can be aspirational, and you can craft it based on how you want to feel and who you aspire to be. But when it comes to actually creating your plan, you'll need to be more specific.

Before we get into how to reverse-engineer to create a plan, here's something to keep in mind: Write stuff down. Whether you're crafting your vision or making a plan, it's better to write it down so it registers in your head.

Reverse-engineering is all about setting your goals. For great outcomes, goals should meet certain qualities, such as being specific and measurable. Additionally, you want goals to have a set deadline. It could be six months, ten years, or twenty-five years from now. Even if you miss your deadline, you'll still figure out if you're moving in the right direction.

Progress is still progress, and you can shift your deadline afterward. But you need to start your investing journey with a deadline set in stone. This will allow you to identify the things that are holding you back from creating your desired outcomes.

Having a timeframe gives you something to work toward. It's essential to constantly remind yourself of the deadline or deadlines in your plan. Write them down every day or at least think about them. Constant reminders keep you on track.

Reverse-engineering the vision of your future will help you plan accordingly. And the great thing about this is that it helps wherever you are on your investing journey.

You could be starting from scratch, and you want to have five properties in your portfolio by this time next year. Or maybe you already have four or five properties and want to double your portfolio in a year or two. Deadlines and clear goals will help you identify what's holding you back. In some cases, it could be your capital, or maybe you're not making good deals. Some are worried about recession and market crashes. Everyone has their own obstacles, but you can't see them clearly unless you know where you're trying to go and how you're going to get there.

That's when you can come up with a game plan to address each problem individually.

Tip No. 4: Obsess, Don't Dabble

You'd think that obsessing about something is bad, but that's not entirely true when you're trying to be a successful investor. When you're crafting a goal or working on your vision, get obsessed with it. Once you set a goal and a deadline, you can't dabble in that goal—you have to be all-in.

That's one of the reasons we recommend writing this stuff down. It's about telling yourself over and over what you're trying to achieve. Your outcome is always in the front of your mind. The chances of getting distracted will be minimal. And there are so many distractions in the world today, and falling off track is easier than you think. You must obsess about your goal to reach your milestones and lifestyle outcomes. Sometimes you might have to make sacrifices along the way.

A few years ago, we used to watch every TV series under the sun. Sound familiar? We know others enjoy this type of entertainment, too. We also realized that it was taking up too much time. Besides, creating and attaining our goals made us more excited than any TV show. So, we pretty much stopped for about two or three years. We saved up to four hours every day by not browsing or watching videos. We became obsessed with meeting our targets, and our sacrifice on the entertainment front gave us the time to do it.

Do you think that's easy to do if you're not passionate about or obsessed with reaching your goal? It isn't.

Obsession enhances your motivation to do what's necessary to secure your desired future. If you only dabble with strategy and investments, you won't have the drive to execute the plan. It will be even harder once you run into some real obstacles. You have to become obsessed and excited about building your future. That's what you need to be willing to create space in your life.

Given most people's circumstances, we know this could sound difficult to achieve. Some people are not naturally obsessive, and that's fine. With practice, you can artificially create obsession around your goals.

Tip No. 5: Set Your KPIs
Key performance indicators (KPIs) are very common in factories, corporations, and many other industries. In essence, KPIs are critical indicators of progress toward a specific, intended result.

Imagine that you set a goal. How do you know you're making progress and you're approaching the desired outcome? You need a measurable value, with "measurable" being the key.

For some people, this might require a slight mindset shift. Working with KPIs is more about having a quantitative perspective instead of a qualitative one. The idea is to figure out a way of quantifying how you're going to measure whether you achieved a set goal, and we do this in a very simple way. This method has shown amazing results when applied to busy professionals looking to get their start in real estate.

One of the most important KPIs is cash flow, which is key for buy-and-hold investors. Another KPI is equity or net worth. This comes down to the amount of equity you have in your properties. It's even more essential if you want to follow a value-add investing strategy. Say you control 1,000 apartment units. That might sound good to say out loud, but you probably wouldn't have 80 to 100 percent equity. As an investor, you need to know exactly what equity you have in your assets (assets are another vital KPI to track).

People often overlook time as a KPI, but it is. Time is a critical indicator of progress toward a goal. Think about it like this—you're a busy professional business owner trying to invest in real estate. If you're like most people who take this path, one of the reasons you want to start investing is to gain back time.

Unfortunately, people don't often track their time. That creates the risk of running your real estate business the same way as everyone else. You'll spend most of your day talking to contractors, getting materials, driving between job sites, and doing a bit of everything else. You wouldn't believe how many investors, especially newbies, do this.

We didn't want to create another nine-to-five for ourselves. That's why we track time as a KPI. The free time we get from setting up a real estate business that runs itself is one way of measuring our progress toward our goals.

Picture the following scenario: You have three to five properties at the moment. By this time next year, you want to double your cash flow, equity, and assets, but you don't want to spend more time working in the business. You can track your free time as you progress toward your goals to determine whether you're taking the right actions. If you're short on time, you probably haven't been making the best decisions. Maybe your strategy needs a tweak, or you need to push your deadlines. We'll break this down more in the chapters to come, but for now, we want you to understand what your KPIs are and why you need to track them.

Once you see free time as a KPI, you'll have a different approach to planning. You'll focus on doing things in the least amount of time and figuring out how to move the needle faster in your business.

This is pretty much automatic for me, especially since I'm a big fan of the 80/20 rule. I'm all about spending 80 percent of the time in the business working on 20 percent of the things in the business. That 20 percent consists of the high-value tasks that generate 80 percent of our return on investment.

Besides, more free time doesn't just increase focus; it also creates ample headspace to think about new business ideas, growth strategies, and more.

Tip No. 6: Work Out How Many Rentals You Need to Retire
Having a comfortable retirement means securing a specific passive income, which can come from the cash flow generated by your portfolio. Say you've crafted your vision. You're motivated, you've set milestones, and you're ready to commit to this journey. You have to ask yourself: How many rentals do I need to retire?

Rental units are income-generating real estate assets. They can help you replicate or exceed your previous income and meet your overall financial objectives.

But remember what we said about goals needing to be tangible? Here's how you put a number to your vision.

Start with your monthly take-home salary after taxes and then divide it by the cash flow generated per each rental unit, and you'll get your answer. Granted, this is the formula in its simplest form. Getting a more accurate number requires working in liabilities, assets, bonuses, debt payments, asset appreciation, and other variables.

However, even a simple formula can give you a good starting point. As you learn more and gain clarity around your goals, you'll be able to fit more variables into the equation. Perhaps you'll want to add childcare or travel expenses. Maybe you're in a higher tax bracket or have other things that dip into your monthly income. Everyone's different, so the formula will be unique to each person's scenario.

The point is that you need to work out the minimum number of rental units your portfolio needs to facilitate your ideal retirement lifestyle. This way, you won't risk stopping growth too soon. Furthermore, suppose you meet your goal ahead of schedule. In that case, you can set higher targets and start working toward building generational wealth and a legacy.

Tip No. 7: Develop a Strategic Plan

Although you may be planning your future and perhaps a retirement that's two decades away, you also need to work on your strategic plan.

Picture this as mapping out various milestones that get you closer to your desired financial and lifestyle outcomes. We recommend doing this on a yearly basis and working from your tangible KPIs. You can divide your year into quarters to break down your big targets into smaller milestones. Then, you can set monthly goals as well and work toward even smaller outcomes.

We use a method to divide the work into sprints and walks. Here's what this looks like:

Imagine setting aside six weeks for heavy-lifting, momentum-building actions. It's a period where you let your obsession take charge and pursue your goals with fervor. Then, you go through a cooling-off period. It's another six-week cycle, but this time you slow down and catch up to the things you started in the first six weeks.

Using this method, you can also create a strategic plan that allows you to set cycles for particular actions. For example, if you're in an acquisition cycle, you can focus your energy and capital on sustaining a buying spree. Once you have enough properties, you can shift your focus to adding value or finding tenants. It's a way of shifting your focus on key areas of your business while giving 100 percent to the things that take you closer to your goal without getting off track.

A strategic plan built from cycles allows you to create and sustain momentum in different business areas, allowing you to better manage and plan using your resources. As your journey progresses, you'll notice that maintaining momentum for extended periods of time is very hard, but a six-week cycle might give you just enough time.

The buying spree is a perfect example. What do investors do when they want to buy properties and nothing else? They look at deals exclusively. However, once they do a deal, they won't start on the next from scratch. They're already doing research and finding many opportunities. This gives you more momentum as opposed to doing a deal today and looking for your next deal two weeks later. But there's another reason why we recommend a strategic plan alternating between sprints and walks, and that's because some people can be very intense when it comes to business.

Personally, we need those walking cycles to force myself to slow down. We can conserve my energy, recharge, and prevent burnout. This might not seem important if you're just starting out as an investor. That said, once you gain knowledge and do a couple of successful deals, you'll start seeing your progression.

Getting a few wins under your belt is enough to boost your confidence, which is great for your overall goals, but it can be harmful if you get carried away and exhaust yourself. Strategic planning will bring a bit of balance in your life as well as focus on what your portfolio needs the most. We recommend doing this for every year, quarter, and month to outline your journey in as much detail as possible.

Tip No. 8: Use the Kickstart Matrix
The Kickstart Matrix is an industry secret, if you will. It comprises three core components, each designed to help you become a better planner for your future. It all starts with making a mindset shift. Most people only focus on what they have to do to get to the place they want to be. Instead, here's what we want you to think about who you have to become to reach your destination.

We've emphasized this before, but it bears repeating: You are your biggest commodity as an investor. While your actions certainly matter, who you are as a person is equally important. This will evolve over time, depending on your overarching goals, capital, and the size of your portfolio.

Now, ask yourself this question: Whose job is it to take me where I need to go? The answer should be you.

This is where ownership, the second core component of the Kickstart Matrix, comes into play. The idea behind this concept is that you must get to a place where you stop blaming and pointing at unfavorable circumstances. It's your job to create favorable circumstances to succeed.

The final element is growth. You know who you have to become. You're also clear that you need to take ownership of that. Then, the only thing that remains is figuring out how to grow into that person. And while you do so, avoid looking at this in terms of productivity. That has nothing to do with it.

THE FUTURE IS YOURS

Many Americans risk retiring without money or a safety net. While it's true that few people receive an adequate financial education, something else could be causing even more harm to people's golden years, and that's inaction.

If you're just starting out as an investor, the idea of building your portfolio is likely more of a fantasy than anything else. You might enjoy the outcomes, but the uncertainty scares you. Your inexperience could prevent you from taking action. These problems plague Americans of all ages. Student debt, expensive bills, and the like force people to live in the present. Most people don't prepare for the future until it's too late to make any significant impact on their financial situation.

But the reality is that you're in charge of your future. If you don't plan and work toward a better tomorrow, no one else will do it for you.

Working a nine-to-five job is consuming enough. Imagine having to do it for another fifteen or thirty years, well into your retirement, only to have barely enough money to get by. Setting yourself up for the future and preparing for retirement should be considered sooner rather than later. Furthermore, you need to plan and outline your journey accordingly if you want to reach your goals.

Leaving the corporate grind to create your financial freedom elsewhere is a great idea. It can offer a lifetime of freedom and satisfaction and even ensure a comfortable retirement—that is, if you do it right.

If you're eager to start this journey, it's time to take action. More

Americans than ever are looking at grim golden years with either little to no savings or working the same job an additional ten to fifteen years. Living a life of freedom will require you to learn a few things—about real estate, finances, and dealing with people. Taking action is just the first step.

You have to take action and seek mentorship and guidance. You need to pull the trigger on getting educated and making the right mindset changes to be a successful investor.

We want you to remember two things: (1) action ahead of perfection, and (2) the future is yours. No one should dictate your potential or set limiting boundaries. You deserve to have more control over your actions and your future.

GOAL SETTING

Often, new investors have a hard time getting started. We developed this formula for anyone who feels stuck and can't figure out how to go from where they are to where they want to go.

Here is the formula you can use to quantify your retirement goals in terms of how many rentals you need to accomplish that goal. We used this formula to decide whether we were ready to quit our jobs.

Retirement Formula

How Many Rentals Do I Need to Retire?

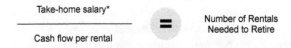

$$\frac{\text{Take-home salary*}}{\text{Cash flow per rental}} = \text{Number of Rentals Needed to Retire}$$

*Remember to use salary after taxes because depreciation offsets taxes for cash flow

The first piece of info you need is your take home salary. We use salary AFTER taxes because (at least in our case), most taxes on our rental income is offset by depreciation. Consult a real estate savvy accountant to ensure that this is accurate for your situation and adjust accordingly. The second piece of information you need is cash flow per rental, which depends on the deal and many other factors. We usually see between $150 and $500, so if you don't have a frame of reference, you can use that range. This will give you the rentals you need to retire with, and this is a range depending on how your income fluctuates and what you use for cash flow, but what this does is it gives you a starting point. This is a very basic formula, so remember: there are a lot of other factors at play (e.g., childcare expenses, tolls, gas, insurance, 401K matching),

If there's still a deficit after doing such a calculation, you can think about and decide if that deficit is worth making this move to build a life for yourself. There is no right or wrong here, and we all have different risk tolerances. Go with what feels right.

This just gives you a starting point and a way to quantify your goals.

ONE-YEAR ROADMAP

By taking our desire to create passive income, wealth, and freedom and putting it into actionable steps, we can turn our desire into results. Unless you have action steps, you're just wanting something without a plan to have it.

One-Year Roadmap

Why?
How?
  Vulnerability
  Comfort Zone

Current status	Where I want to be 1 year from now
Why are these goals important?	What capabilities do I need to achieve these goals?

Before we dive in, there are two things I want to talk about. The first is "why," and this is the most important question you will ask yourself. Why are we doing this? In my (Palak's) case, my drive came from a visceral need to be with my kids, and no formula or analysis could convince me otherwise. You need to know why you're setting out to invest in real estate, and then the "how" is what you figure out. And if your "why" is strong, if your first how doesn't work, you'll try another way. And keep going as long as your "why" is strong enough to motivate you to not give up.

Take a piece of paper and draw a cross in the middle. Put down your current status in the top left corner. For example, you might write, "I have two rental properties and I want to scale to ten." On the top right, put down where do you want to be a year from now. For example, "I want to set up a foundation to be able to grow with systems, teams, and processes in place." And then on the bottom left, write down why this is important. This is what's going to keep moving you forward when you hit a roadblock. For example, you might write, "I want financial freedom so I can take care of my family better." Last, on the bottom right, you'll address what capabilities you'll need to achieve these goals. When we get done, you can finish this bottom right section. It will end up being something like Deal Analysis, Finance, Property Management—whatever capabilities you figure out you need.

One piece of advice I have for you is this is the time to step out of your comfort zone and be vulnerable. Accept what you don't know, and celebrate what you do know.

To help you build your investor brand, craft your vision, reverse-engineer your retirement, and define an action plan so you can take tangible steps to reach financial freedom, we have created a free five-day pop-up challenge at www.biggerpockets.com/acceleratebonus.

Fast Forward

Five years after we started investing, it is a typical Wednesday morning. We're getting our children (7 and 5 years old) ready for school, making breakfast, packing lunches, and dressing while "Raining Tacos" plays in the background—you know, the usual weekday with young kids.

Niti is making two-egg omelets with cheese, "extra-golden," just as our kids like it. In some ways, our lives look the same.

But our lives have changed tremendously. Once the kids go off to school, we will walk over to our home office with coffee and start our morning routine. We'll clean off our giant white board and start with vision and strategy before moving over to our daily tasks to execute. Some days we work eight hours and some days we barely work thirty minutes. But it doesn't matter. It's our choice. And our business continues to grow due to the power of the SCALE framework.

Yes, it took many mindset shifts, many uncomfortable spurts of growth, many lessons learned as CEOs of our business. It was not an easy path, but we get to grow the business at our pace without compromising time with our kids.

Now, no one tells us how to spend our time and what our growth potential is. We still like to work hard, because that's how we are built. But now, that hard work grows wealth for our children instead of for our employer. Our work helps other investors achieve the same freedom that we have instead of improving the bottom line for some large corporation.

That makes us feel that we are truly in control of our own destinies. And that is all we ever wanted.

Acknowledgments

We would like to express our deepest gratitude to everyone who has contributed to this work. First and foremost, we'd like to thank our kids for their patience as we worked through this book. We'd also like to thank the team at BiggerPockets, who worked tirelessly to make this book the best it could be. Their insights, guidance, and expertise were invaluable, and we could not have done it without them.

Finally, we would like to thank our readers for their interest and enthusiasm. Writing a book is a labor of love, and it means the world to us that so many people have found value in our work.

Thank you all for your support, encouragement, and belief in us. We are honored to have had the opportunity to write this book, and we hope it will be of value to all who read it.

About the Authors

After more than fifteen years in corporate America, Palak Shah and Niti Jamdar left their jobs to create a multi-million-dollar real estate rental portfolio within a three-year time period. They leveraged systems, processes, capital, teams, and an anti-DIY approach to buy assets and replicate their nine-to-five income. They have helped hundreds of real estate investors generate millions in assets. They live with their two beautiful children outside of Philadelphia and invest in various locations throughout the U.S.

Thank You

Thank you for reading Accelerate Your Real Estate!

We know you're on the path to breaking free from the golden handcuffs and living the life of your dreams. We applaud you for taking the first step and want to support you as much as possible on your journey.

If you enjoyed this book, we hope you'll take a moment to check out some of the other great material BiggerPockets offers. Whether you crave freedom or stability, a backup plan, or passive income, BiggerPockets empowers you to live life on your own terms through real estate investing. You can also head over to www.openspaceswomen.com for access to free resources and blogs and to find out how we can help you implement proven strategies that will move you closer to your goals.

If you're interested in working with our team and learning more about how to turn $25,000 into a $1 million portfolio, email us at (info@openspacescapital.com).

SUPERCHARGE YOUR REAL ESTATE INVESTING.

Get **exclusive bonus content** like checklists, contracts, interviews, and more when you buy from the BiggerPockets Bookstore.

Real Estate by the Numbers: A Complete Reference Guide to Deal Analysis
by J Scott and Dave Meyer

From cash flow to compound interest, *Real Estate by the Numbers* makes it easy for anyone to master real estate deal analysis.
www.biggerpockets.com/bythenumbers

Buy, Rehab, Rent, Refinance, Repeat
by David Greene

The five-part BRRRR real estate investing strategy makes financial freedom more attainable than ever, and this book shows you how.
www.biggerpockets.com/brrrrbook

The Book on Estimating Rehab Costs
by J Scott

How much does it really cost to flip a house? In this new second edition, get all the updated costs, upgrade details, and associated values to estimate your next renovation!
www.biggerpockets.com/rehabbook

The Book on Tax Strategies for the Savvy Real Estate Investor
by Amanda Han & Matt MacFarland

Powerful techniques real estate investors can use to deduct more, invest smarter, and pay far less to the IRS!
www.biggerpockets.com/taxbook

Use code **FirstBPBook** for **15%** off your first purchase.

Standard shipping is free and
you get bonus content with every order!

www.BiggerPockets.com/STORE

Looking for more?
Join the BiggerPockets Community

BiggerPockets brings together education, tools, and a community of more than 2+ million like-minded members—all in one place. Learn about investment strategies, analyze properties, connect with investor-friendly agents, and more.

Go to **biggerpockets.com** to learn more!

 Listen to a **BiggerPockets Podcast**

 Watch **BiggerPockets on YouTube**

 Join the **Community Forum**

 Learn more on **the Blog**

 Read more **BiggerPockets Books**

 Learn about our **Real Estate Investing Bootcamps**

 Connect with an **Investor-Friendly Real Estate Agent**

 Go Pro! Start, scale, and manage your portfolio with your **Pro Membership**

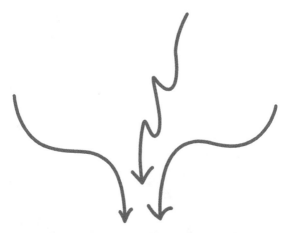

Follow us on social media!

Sign up for a Pro account and take **20 PERCENT OFF** with code **BOOKS20**.

 BiggerPockets®

Printed in the USA
CPSIA information can be obtained
at www.ICGtesting.com
LVHW011658241223
767353LV00018B/1449